Next Practices

An Executive Guide for Education Decision Makers

Darryl Vidal and Michael Casey

ROWMAN & LITTLEFIELD EDUCATION

A division of
ROWMAN & LITTLEFIELD
Lanham • Boulder • New York • Toronto • Plymouth, UK

Published by Rowman & Littlefield Education
A division of Rowman & Littlefield
4501 Forbes Boulevard, Suite 200, Lanham, Maryland 20706
www.rowman.com

10 Thornbury Road, Plymouth PL6 7PP, United Kingdom

British Library Cataloguing in Publication Information Available

Library of Congress Cataloging-in-Publication Data
Vidal, Darryl, 1963– author.
  Next practices : an executive guide for education decision makers / Darryl Vidal and Michael Casey.
     pages cm
  Includes index.
  ISBN 978-1-4758-0800-1 (cloth : alk. paper) — ISBN 978-1-4758-0801-8 (pbk. : alk. paper) — ISBN 978-1-4758-0802-5 (electronic) 1. Educational technology. 2. School management and organization—United States—Decision making. I. Casey, Michael, 1957– author. II. Title.
  LB1028.3.V52 2014
  371.33—dc23   2013040689

Printed in the United States of America

Contents

Introduction

Next Practices is a ground-breaking advisory book for education decision makers. Its purpose is to challenge the top trends and initiatives of the previous decade in education technology and bring light to their shortfalls and misses. It also highlights successful endeavors and strategies, and details a commonsense methodology to move your school/ district forward in its technology initiatives while ensuring sustainability, longevity, and, ultimately, success through results.

Next Practices identifies technology-based initiatives, such as interactive white boards, data centers, and one-to-one computing, and reviews actual implementations and case studies—both successful and unsuccessful—to provide a structure to plan and implement education-technology initiatives practical for schools and districts of all sizes.

Next Practices goes beyond the examination of current best practices and redefines for educational leaders *next* practices for successful technology initiatives in support of 21st-century learning.

The authors of *Next Practices* are real-world educational technology practitioners with over twenty years of experience each working with technology in K–12 education.

CHAPTER 1

Education Technology as Defined

INTRODUCTION

As we are charged with the task of preparing students for the 21st century (and we better hurry up since it's already here), it is important to first of all reflect on what 21st-century skills are, and perhaps more important, reflect on what they are not!

Preparing students for the 21st century is not about buying the latest technology gadget, nor is it about acquiring technology for technology's sake. It's about blending the core subjects of reading, writing, and mathematics with learning and innovation skills (creativity and innovation, critical thinking and problem solving, and communication and collaboration); information, media, and technology skills (information literacy, media literacy, and technology literacy); and life and career skills.

As we engage in discussions with superintendents and board members about 21st-century skills and how to help students achieve those skills, the topic always seems to very quickly move toward questions about what folks are doing with technology.

"So when are you going to put a one-to-one program in your district?"

"Are you going to provide computers to all of your students?"

"Are you getting electronic white boards for all your classrooms?"

The concern we have is that folks are not asking the right questions. The real questions we need to ask ourselves, when we are trying to implement *Next* Practices, should be about curriculum, not about technology.

These are questions we try to avoid because they are more difficult to address. For example,

"What methodologies do you practice and model to support the writing process at your school district?"

"How are students in your school district presenting, collaborating, and making public their work?"

Oh sure, pretty much anyone in a decision-making capacity, or a member of the board of education, can recite what 21st-century skills are, but rarely will you get any kind of a detailed or focused answer about what a school site or district is doing with curriculum and how their curriculum focus is aligned with 21st-century learning.

Having a strongly focused curriculum that supports 21st-century learning is the most important factor that will guide you in the use of supporting technology tools. *Having a strongly focused curriculum that you can articulate clearly to everyone* is a *Next* Practice. Until you can clearly define what your curriculum focus is and how you are going to support that particular focus, you are not ready to look at technology solutions.

This book will debate the value of technology solutions that have emerged in the past decade and whether or not they support 21st-century learning.

Case Number 1

A school district recently purchased iPads for the students in 4th–6th grade throughout their district. They spent thousands and thousands of dollars on this project. The education technology director was very excited when talking about this project, saying how excited the students would be and what a cool technology this was and bragging about what wonderful things kids could do with their new iPads. I had to bring up the question "Hey, what applications on these new iPads support your curriculum focus?"

The education technology director replied, "Well, we're still looking for apps that we can use."

My reply: "Interesting, I'm sure you'll find something that you can use."

I continued my questions.

"How are you going to support these new iPads? What tools or strategy are you using to manage and/or sync these?"

His response: "We're still figuring that out."

Surprisingly, this is not an unusual scenario. It is quite often that a school or district gets distracted with the purchase of a new technology that's cool and fun to use. But to be effective with any technology, the school or district must support instruction first and foremost.

There is a balance, however. Although technology should be introduced as part of a curriculum and professional development plan, we have all seen, sometimes daily, astounding examples of teachers and students creating phenomenal examples of project-based and collaborative-work projects using technology when this process wasn't followed. That is to say, the introduction of technology without a specific and detailed plan may still produce a positive curricular impact. The questions then become

1. How do we evaluate the effectiveness of these activities?
2. Do these types of activities support the instructional program?
3. Can this curriculum be "packaged" as a professional development curriculum for the other teachers in the school/district? and
4. Does the technology infrastructure and end-user device platform scale along with the curriculum?

As we reflect on the last decade, we will examine technologies that have been both "hits" and "misses." Keep in mind that our frame of reference is whether or not a technology truly supports 21st-century learning and how it might support the curriculum efforts of your school district.

The following chapters will outrage some, reaffirm others (that they are on the right track), and seem like heresy to yet others. These are our opinions based on over twenty years of using, implementing, and evaluating classroom technologies.

As we begin this journey, I am reminded of a quote from Albert Einstein: "Great spirits have always encountered violent opposition from mediocre minds."

EDUCATION AND TECHNOLOGY

These words go together like biscuits and gravy, yet schools are plagued by insufficient understanding of one area by the other. This comparison works both ways: most educators don't have a deep understanding of technology or how it all hangs together, while technologists don't understand education from the educator's perspective. This conceptual divide typically results in the following outcomes.

1. Money spent on technology without specific curricular planning—meaning little or no resultant benefit to student learning or academic results, or a result that can't be measured by a means that is reliable and defensible.
2. Technology that cannot be used effectively because of lack of infrastructure.
3. Technology in the classroom that the teacher hasn't been trained to use effectively from both a technological standpoint as well as from an integration into curriculum perspective.

This isn't apparent except to those who actually evaluate these programs and can view education-technology implementations from an objective standpoint, or to those who have been privy to funding technology initiatives, only to see the technology go unused and students who don't derive any real benefit from the technology.

Technology doesn't exist only in the classroom. In fact, in any technology initiative (executed properly), a larger percentage of investment occurs in infrastructure, such as cabling and networking equipment and wireless—and professional development will need to be budgeted as part of the technology initiative.

Technology directors in education must strike a balance with technology implementation funding: how to properly fund infrastructure while providing a measure of impact in the classroom and providing tools and methods for professional development. Thus we can identify three tiers that assist us in identifying education-technology success.

1. Infrastructure—How does all of this hang together?
2. Classroom technology—What is the impact on student achievement?
3. Sustainability—How do I keep it? Do they know how to use it?

As we examine technology initiatives from the last decade, we will refer to these three tiers for measuring success and defining *Next Practices* for the 21st-century classroom.

Sustainability becomes an overlay of all the processes, practices, and resources that support the maintenance and operations of technology systems over time. This includes hardware warranties, software support, information-technology support, education-technology support, and professional development.

The biggest implementation mistake is to undertake one area without considering the cost of the other two, or worse, to undertake implementation in tier 2 (classroom technology), without sufficient tier 1 (infrastructure) and tier 3 (sustainability) resources. This mistake can be seen repeated over and over in schools and districts large and small.

Think of the parent foundation that purchased computers for classrooms, with no software or networking—or how about the widespread purchase of tablet devices, with no applications that are directly connected to curriculum initiatives or a method to manage them?

Through examples, this book will provide the basis for planning a technology initiative, identifying the common mistakes and stumbling blocks typically encountered, and offering valuable and insightful anecdotes that will help executive decision-makers and education technologists navigate the twists and turns of technology implementation in the classroom and, ultimately, their positive impact on student achievement.

YOUR ORGANIZATION

In any planning methodology, the first thing to do is an in-depth assessment of the current state of affairs—this is a planning best practice. In regards to education technology, this includes an honest assessment of all things technology oriented. More specifically, within the district organization are two discrete entities, or, better stated, roles. These roles may, in a small district, be performed by one individual, or they may, in a very large school district, be completely separate organizations. Let's look at the roles, and then we'll look at organizational examples.

First, a couple of definitions.

- *Education technology*—the role of supporting teaching using technology tools.
- *Information technology services*—the role of installing, managing, and maintaining technology infrastructure, including managing

business applications that support the organization; for example, e-mail, finance, procurement, human resources, and so forth.

The evolving district organization has seen varying examples of managing these roles within the district administration. Variances are revealed not in the size of the organization, but in the philosophical, hierarchical, and administrative implementations.

Information Technology versus Education Technology

The legacy organizational structure relative to technology typically looks like figure 1.1.

In this example, we see the information technology (IT) department as a support-and-maintenance operation within the business department—traditionally the home of IT because of capital and procurement needs that fall under the business department, and the support for the business applications.

There is nothing inherently wrong with this structure.

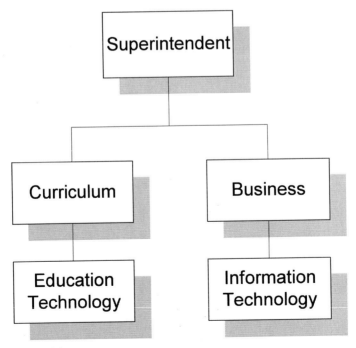

Figure 1.1

However, technology needs aren't necessarily raised to the cabinet level.

In figure 1.2, we see the more modern organization that raises technology to the cabinet level, bringing visibility of technology initiatives to leadership. This shifts technology to a strategic part of the district rather than a support organization.

In figure 1.3, we can see the arising dilemma. It is fairly typical for the education-technology role to emerge from within the curriculum department. Teachers on special assignment, technology teachers, and media specialists take on these roles.

As the departments grow, their independence may foster isolation within their hierarchy and inhibit collaboration with "bureaucrats." Education technologists say, "Those techies don't know anything about teaching kids." The IT guys say, "They're teachers, they have no idea how any of this really works."

Without disciplined collaboration between leadership at the cabinet level, the organizations act independently—Read: *The right hand doesn't know what the left hand is doing.*

Reports are published, plans documented, and budgets approved without vetting by the other technology departments. Education Technology staffers take the sides of teachers and curricular priorities, while IT focuses on standards, network management, and enterprise IT concerns. Focus on the student and learning remains in the classroom.

I'm reminded of a district where there was zero interaction between education technology and IT. Not only did they work against each other, but their clientele also demonized their supposed support organizations.

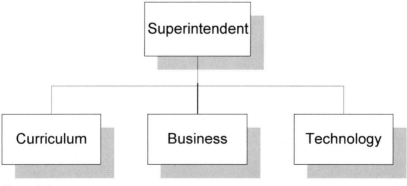

Figure 1.2.

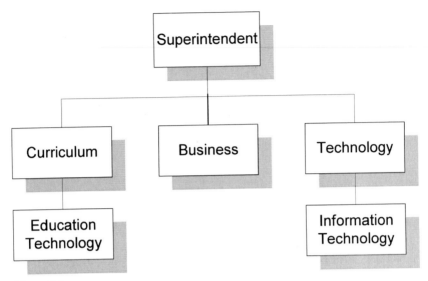

Figure 1.3.

Help-desk tracking functions and training were never aligned. Consultants were used to foster communication between the organizations.

Figure 1.4 depicts the evolution of the technology organization within the curriculum organization. Although this organization lacks a cabinet-level technology head, the curriculum leader takes on this role.

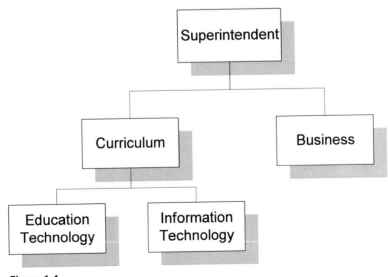

Figure 1.4.

There is no one perfect model. Your organization will take on a structure based on your size and the expertise within your organization. Later in this book we will take a deep dive and examine the various roles that must exist within these organizations.

Next Practices involve *technology at the cabinet level to ensure that technology is strategic to the organization* and not as just a maintenance organization.

CHAPTER 2

Real-World Technology Successes and Failures—What and Why

INTERACTIVE WHITE BOARDS

An interactive white board (IWB) is a touch input device that allows a user to touch on a white board surface to click on an object, resize, scroll, or run an application, rather than click a mouse. During the last decade, IWBs have been installed in classrooms by the thousands. If you walk into these classrooms, you will see the same disparity in usage that you would for almost any technology—some teachers use them effectively, and some don't.

The success or failure of your IWB initiative will be just like it sounds: If it is an IWB initiative (meaning that the initiative is simply about the technology), then it can only be successful as far as getting a large percentage of your teachers using the technology as defined by the manufacturer's professional development, and your district's investment in professional development. The good news is there is really no quantifiable "failure" to be measured, just as there can be little objective measure of "success" except for student achievement and test scores—and independent studies don't seem to support this.

From our experience installing IWBs in classrooms for over ten years, we strain to see a significant increase in academic achievement.

Reading/language arts and mathematics achievement test scores of all students in the third through eighth grades in a small urban school district in northern Ohio were compared between students whose teachers used interactive whiteboards for instruction and those whose teachers did not. A statistically significant but not meaningful positive main effect of whiteboard use on mathematics achievement was found. A statistically significant main effect on reading achievement was not found, although the reading/language arts scores of students whose teachers used whiteboards were slightly higher than those of students whose teachers did not use them. In addition, statistically significant and meaningful interactions between whiteboard use and grade levels were found, leading to a more careful look at differences in the ways teachers employed whiteboards in their instruction. A within-group comparison of such usage between teachers whose students scored above the mean on standardized tests and those whose students scored at or below the mean revealed that teachers of high-scoring students used interactive whiteboards more frequently and in more creative and constructivist ways than did teachers whose students performed at or below the mean. The results suggest that the use of interactive whiteboards can enhance student learning of mathematics and reading/language arts when teachers use them in a manner that takes advantage of their unique capabilities. (Swan, K., Kratcoski, A., Schenker, J., & van 't Hooft, M. [in press]. "Interactive Whiteboards and Student Achievement." In Thomas, M., and Schmid, E. C. [Eds.], *Interactive Whiteboards for Education and Training: Emerging Technologies and Applications*. Hershey, PA: IGI Global)

Unfortunately, the data simply do not demonstrate that the compelling nature of the technology increases student achievement reflected through test scores. It does seem to show that teachers using more creative and constructive techniques do have an effect on achievement, just as creativity and constructive techniques would without IWBs.

In another study,

the researcher studied the effects of the implementation of IWBs on Georgia's end-of-course test (EOCT) scores and satisfaction of students with this method of instruction. The researcher compared EOCT scores of a Georgia high school the year before and after IWBs were used. A satisfaction survey was also developed and used to evaluate if students were satisfied with being instructed with IWBs. Based on the results, students were satisfied with this type of instruction. However, only one academic area resulted in improved test scores. Overall, the results of the study do not support the use of IWBs. ("Effects of Instruction with Interactive Whiteboards versus Instruction without Interactive Whiteboards on End-of-Course Test Scores, " Evans, Kendra J., dissertation, Trevecca Nazarene College)

Installing IWBs—or any other technology—will not trigger higher achievement. It would then hold that once again, the key is in execution—meaning professional development connected to a well-defined curriculum. Installing IWBs district-wide and having students and teachers love them still is a benefit, right? But is it cost justified?

Pedagogical Shift via the IWB

The Sage on the Stage, or the Guide on the Side, or the
Teacher Talking to the White Board

Although use of an IWB may prove more enjoyable for the teacher and student, anecdotes don't seem to support a pedagogical shift in teaching techniques triggered by the installation of IWBs. In fact, it seems to trigger the opposite effect.

One of the functional challenges with the IWB is that it places the teacher back into the traditional model of "talking to the wall." When I was in grade school (forty years ago) I can recall the teacher using a presentation technique of writing on the board without speaking, then dutifully turning to the class and establishing eye contact with students while presenting, then pointing back at, key words, sentences, and drawings on the board—a presentation model reinforced by the IWB. This model can be aided with the installation of an audio amplification system with a teacher microphone. It may not achieve the personal interaction of eye contact, but you can certainly blast your voice throughout the classroom while keeping your back to the students.

Some educators contend that at the elementary level, students are drawn to interaction with the board. It rewards participation, and it emphasizes speaking and presentation skills.

I saw a great example of a first-grade classroom where the teacher would have the students perform math exercises with the IWB using an arithmetic "game." The students took turns getting up on a small kitchen step-stool that the teacher brought from home so they could reach the board. Hmmm.

To bring the board to the appropriate height level for K–2 students, the board can be mounted on a height-adjustable mount. Hmmm.

I recently surveyed math and science teachers who received technology classrooms we built back in 2008. After four years of using the suite of technology in the classroom, they were asked, "I'm looking for descriptions of significant impact to instructional techniques precipitated by the classroom technology."

Here is one response: "I would say that on the whole the new classroom technology actually has not yet precipitated a significant impact to instructional techniques. I say this because:

1) Only some of the teachers make regular use of the technology beyond the whiteboard and document camera.
2) Most of the use that does occur is not significantly different from what already occurred in the previous classrooms. For example, though definitely an improvement, these do not represent radically significant pedagogical shifts:
   a. Interactive white board vs. chalk board
   b. Document camera vs. overhead projector—way more versatile and great to have, yes, but not a significant pedagogical shift." Michel Paul, math teacher.

Big Screens, Big Kids, and Big Images

The height limitation issue comes up again, especially in secondary environments—average height for adults is still under six feet tall—thereby limiting the height the board can be mounted in the standard classroom.

In one of my projects, we had giant science classrooms with twelve-foot ceilings. By using twelve-foot-wide screens mounted high on the wall, the giant projected image could be viewed by all students throughout the classroom, above the heads of the students (who are mostly adult-size by high school).

Sitting among Them

One of my most successful technology classroom implementations saw the teacher sitting in the back of the room among the students, speaking into a classroom amplification system using a wireless slate and manipulating images on the big screen. She was able to sit among her students, speaking in a soft voice. Now that's interactivity, but not with the wall—with the students.

Software Communities

Next time you see an IWB demonstration, ask yourself, *Am I watching a great hardware demo, or a great software demo?*

Yes, interacting with the white board is fun and whiz-bang, but once the demo gets to real content and tools, you'll notice that it's really not the white board that's adding the most value, it's the software and the online communities filled with pre-made content.

I helped a school district document several evaluations of competing white boards and their associated software tools. The competing hardware platforms were almost identical—one was more robust in construction, the other had a larger installed base. Besides, if there is something new in hardware, just take a few breaths, and it will be different and better before you hyperventilate. As a perfect example, within months of this study, new technologies were introduced by both manufacturers that made both platforms obsolete.

Then it came to the software evaluation. Depending on what factors were being compared, each could be rated differently compared with the other (this is a phenomenon we consultants refer to as "outcome flexibility"). Basically, the consultant can *define and/or organize* the rating categories to favor one solution over the other. This is especially easy to do when comparing subjective factors like ease-of-use, functionality, and intuitiveness.

Math demonstrations are particularly impressive because most productivity software and the standard keyboard don't support all the symbols and flexibility required to do equations, proofs, graphs, and so forth. The presenters click away to their user community and pull from literally hundreds of pre-made curricular presentations that have been developed by others—slam dunk—sold another white board.

A 2009 article in *National Education Association Member Benefits* states the following:

Classroom applications for using interactive whiteboards include:

- Multimedia lessons and presentations including audio and video
- Collaborative problem solving
- Showcasing student projects and presentations
- Virtual field trips

- Recorded lessons that can be used by substitute teachers
- Documentation of student achievement

("Interactive Whiteboards Enhance Classroom Instruction and Learning," Teich, A., May 13, 2009.)

Unfortunately, this list doesn't seem to include anything that actually requires an IWB.

Conclusion: *Buying expensive technologies without providing specific curricular objectives and focused professional development for use* is not a *Next* Practice.

ONE-TO-ONE INITIATIVES

When school districts mention one-to-one projects or initiatives, a number of questions come to mind. First, what do you mean by one-to-one? Does that mean every student has a computer or some type of device that they carry around with them all day? Does the technology stay in the classroom? Does every classroom have a one-to-one ratio of technology devices to students? Or does it mean that when I need every student to use a technology, that technology is available to them in a one-to-one environment? Are we buying laptops, Netbooks, tablets, Kindles, Chromebooks, graphing calculators, iPod Touches, smart phones, or whatever the latest gizmo is?

There is no one correct model for one-to-one initiatives. The answer is, it depends! We believe that one-to-one initiatives that fail to meet their desired outcomes weren't clearly defined before the initiative was started. Unless, of course, the objective was merely to just put technology in the hands of students, assuming they would figure it out from there. That is a typical case of "a solution looking for a problem."

Successful one-to-one implementations start in a different way. In fact, we abhor the use of the phrase "one-to-one"—it implies the idea that this is all about the technology and not about what students will be able to achieve by having access to technology. So let's describe how a successful initiative is accomplished. Don't worry, we'll get to the gadgets soon enough.

To begin, examine what your curriculum goals are for your district for the next two to three years, the specific, tangible, actionable objectives that you want to focus on, and objectives that you believe technology may help you achieve. Focus on a few. It is better to do one thing really well than to try and do a lot of things not so well.

Once you can articulate your curriculum focus, then it is time for you to explore which technologies might be effective in supporting your curriculum focus. The key point is that *you now have a curriculum initiative and not a technology initiative.*

Let us continue to examine what we mean by a one-to-one curriculum initiative that integrates technology well. A perfect example of a 21st-century learning tool is Google Docs.

Google Docs for Education

Google Docs originated from two separate products, Writely and Google Spreadsheets. Writely was a Web-based word processor created by the software company Upstartle that was launched in August 2005. Google Spreadsheets launched as Google Labs Spreadsheets on June 6, 2006. Writely's original features included a collaborative text-editing suite and some form of access control. The menus, keyboard shortcuts, and dialog boxes were similar to what users might expect in a desktop word processor such as Microsoft Word. In February 2007, Google Docs was made available to Google Apps users.

Google Apps allows students to communicate and collaborate in a shared environment using online documents, calendaring, and Web publishing. Students are able to securely upload, access, share, and work with documents from any computer connected to the Internet using Google Apps.

National Educational Technology Standards for all students in grades K–12 stress the importance of collaboration and communication among students locally as well as on a global level. Twenty-first-century skills in communication and collaboration are also strongly supported by the use of Google Apps. Google Apps allows students to demonstrate mastery of those standards while providing collaborative tools to students and teachers.

Google Apps supports effective writing with built-in tools for creating, collaborating, revising, and publishing. Google Docs supports online interaction, promoting the transition from paper-based development, input, and feedback to true collaboration. Students move beyond paper drafts and waiting for teachers to complete physical edits. Online comments and real-time editing let students see comments as they come in from their teachers and peers, the students then acting on them and streamlining the writing process. Teachers can provide feedback electronically whenever it is important in the revision cycle. *Providing students tools to support 21st-century learning*—definitely a *Next* Practice.

Case Number 2

I recently visited a fourth-grade classroom in southern California. The focus of the school district is clearly defined, and all of the teachers are focused on writing and the writing process. In the particular classroom that I was in, each student had his or her own laptop to use. When I asked why these students each had their own technology tool, the teacher related to me that they were part of a curriculum pilot group that was testing a tool that supported their curriculum efforts (writing process) and that Google Docs was the application they used to support the writing process. Not once was the term "one-to-one computing" used. The focus was on tools that supported their curriculum and not about technology. The teacher went on to explain how Google Docs supported the writing process. She went into great detail about how the use of collaboration between peer students, her use of comments, and even the chat feature supported the writing efforts of her students. The students in her class could work and collaborate on their writing from any computer that had a modern browser and could connect to the Internet. Her students were more prolific in their writing, their vocabulary had improved, and they enjoyed writing much more than in classes not using Google Docs.

Recently her students had had a writing assignment where they were teamed up with a partner for their assignment. Each team member was to contribute to the same document, but with each using his or her own laptop. To accomplish this, one member of the team created a new document in Google Docs. Then they shared the document with their other team member, giving them full editing privileges. Voila, the students were able to coauthor the same document. Later that week, one of the girls in the class had to go to the hospital for an injury she had suffered. She was upset that she would not be able to participate with her team member on the assignment. With minimal communication with her mother, she was able to log on to Google Docs from the hospital and participate in the assignment!

Using tools that support collaboration in a meaningful way is a *Next* Practice.

Let's return to our discussion about one-to-one curriculum initiatives that integrate technology. We recently surveyed a number of teachers who are integrating technology into their curriculum in an environment where every student has their own wireless device that supports their curriculum focus of writing and the writing process. We asked the teachers, "How is your classroom different than before? What changes have you noticed in your teaching? What changes have you noticed in your students?" The responses we received can be summarized.

- Easier-to-read student work
- Higher level of teacher-student comments about students' writing
- Much more frequent comments between teacher and student
- More time for teachers' comments
- More prolific student writing
- Use of higher-level vocabulary (million-dollar words instead of five-dollar words)
- "Easy" writing process; rewrites not "painful"

The technical analysis of these results highlights a particular "old school" pedagogy—collaboration between the teacher and student—that of submission, assessment, feedback, and revision. In fact, in the "manual" method, the student turned in homework, and the teacher graded it—submission and assessment. In writing classes, the feedback and revision process is taught. But what if the transaction time is reduced to instantaneous? Using collaborative applications, the feedback and submission process can be repeated over and over—with each and every student. It is the iterative nature of the teacher-student interaction that increases student understanding and refinement of these skills. That means it all comes down to transaction time: technology tools that support the ability of the teacher to participate in multiple conversations, with multiple students, in a very short period of time have an immediate and long-lasting impact on student learning.

Today, everyone uses e-mail and texting. This "store-and-forward" technology has significant advantages over traditional synchronous models. Since feedback is immediate, teacher-student response times can be reduced, but since the conversation is available "after the fact," nothing is lost after the interaction—such as the student yawning during the salient part of a lecture.

As a result of this exercise, we have come to a profound new belief. One-to-one implementation is not about one student, one device. *One-to-one is about one teacher to one student.* It's about the number of times during the day a teacher has meaningful contact with a child, whether it be a text-type message, a comment exchange in Google Docs, or a face-to-face encounter. What technology and Google Docs have done is provide a means that will create extra time for a teacher to have more contact with an individual child!

Now is the moment to engage with the technology professionals within your district, whether that is the technology director (in a small district), or both the education technology manager and the information technology manager (in a larger district). With knowledge of your curriculum focus, you will work together as a team to determine what technologies support your initiative.

Once you have selected technology that you think will best support your curriculum project, it is a good idea to pilot the technology in a few classrooms at different grade levels to ensure that the technology will, in reality, support your curriculum project.

This is also a perfect time for your technology department to evaluate whether or not they are ready to support such an initiative if rolled out to an entire school/district. And it is an opportunity to develop and fine-tune the professional development activities that will be essential to a successful project.

Let's tackle the technology issues first. Most likely the technology you have chosen is one that uses wireless technology to connect to your network and the Internet. The LANs and WLANs (local area networks and wireless local area networks) of most schools are unprepared to support more than thirty-three devices in each classroom. Wireless classroom devices will require a network that provides wireless saturation not just wireless coverage.

Your technology department will need to investigate what will be required to build a saturated wireless environment and where it will be needed. (Do you need saturated wireless on the playing fields, in your music classes, or on the quad? Maybe, it depends on your curriculum focus.)

Your technology department will also need to ensure that the structured cabling is capable of supporting any additional wireless infrastructure, and that power and rack space for any additional wireless infrastructure is available. You don't want to have a failure to launch because your infrastructure is not capable of handling all of the added capacity you are about to throw at it! It is essential that you plan and budget to implement infrastructure improvements to ensure that you can support the additional devices on the network. The other area that you will want your technology department to help with is recommending how to store and charge the devices in a classroom. Are the devices going to be stored in carts? Will some kind of special casework be built? Or will the students just carry them in their backpacks and be responsible for storing and charging their technology at home?

Having done a pilot will greatly decrease your risk and will give you an opportunity to work out all of your potential technology issues.

Now let's tackle professional development. Even though you are deploying technology as part of your curriculum initiative, *most* of your professional development needs to be about curriculum and how technology as a tool is integrated. Teachers will need to spend some time learning about the technology and the classroom management of the technology; however, we estimate that 85 percent of professional development activities need to be focused on curriculum. If you have an education-technology department, this is where they can best assist. They understand technologies and how to manage and support them in a classroom environment. They need to work hand in hand with your curriculum experts to develop professional development activities that will support your initiative. Once again, doing a pilot gives you a chance to kick the tires on your professional development activities, ensuring success as you roll out your initiative.

Speaking of rolling out your curriculum initiative, you need to have a rollout plan. Your curriculum department and your technology department must work together to devise a plan for deploying and supporting the technology that is supporting your curriculum project. How will you deploy 1,000, 2,000, or even more devices successfully?

One last item to address is a review of your board policy and acceptable use policy to ensure they are current and reflect the use and responsibility of any new technologies.

Curriculum initiatives that incorporate technology in a meaningful way and are not simply one-to-one initiatives are a *Next* Practice.

WIRELESS NETWORKING

As we look to the future and attempt to imagine what the world of technology will look like 3 . . . 5 . . . 7 years from now, one certainty is that network infrastructure will be the most critical component in delivering solutions to the classroom. It is our belief that endpoints will become devices that merely connect you to the network, and all services will be delivered to those endpoints. Déjà vu! Sounds like the 1970s model of mainframe computing and terminals! The only difference is that we have made it really cool and wireless! Users will have access to the same resources no matter where they are—ubiquitous computing will actually become a reality.

Metropolitan networks will be required to deliver services to satellite sites within an organization. Bandwidth must be taken out of the equation for the delivery model to be successful. Networks will need to be self-healing, self-defending, resilient, and reliable.

Whatever future endpoints might be, they will be wireless!

Intelligent wireless will be critical to the success of any initiative where every student has their own wireless device. If students can't get on the network, they cannot be successful in integrating your focused curriculum.

Why do I need a wired network and this entire wired infrastructure if all of my devices are going to be wireless? Well, let's take a moment to understand how wireless networks actually work. Wireless devices connect to your "wired" network through a wireless access point (AP). APs are essentially radios. Yep, just like the walkie-talkie radios that you used as a kid. Those radios (APs) are connected to a switch. The switch is connected to a router, and the router directs the communication from the AP to a wireless controller. The wireless controller manages the APs on your network. Whew!

So you can see there is a lot more to a wireless network then just hanging up APs. There are many shortcuts, but beware, shortcuts will almost always lead to disaster. It is better to build a robust wireless network that is capable of expansion. You still need a robust, "wired" backbone. That doesn't go away.

A school district in California embarked on a "pilot" program that used handheld wireless devices. In the pilot, three classroom teachers were chosen, and each child in those classrooms had their own wireless device. The pilot went extremely well. Kids were excited, parents were excited, test scores in those classrooms were showing measured improvement, and the technology teacher along with the classroom teacher were on cloud nine. So with little convincing, the pilot became a school-wide initiative. Funding was acquired to buy hundreds of devices; teachers spent the summer training; the curriculum was aligned and focused; and all of the kids were excited that they were joining their fellow classmates in using this new technology. When the students all went to connect their wireless devices—you can guess what happened—yep, a failure to launch. Bummer! Their current wireless network failed them. They had an older wireless network that was really a hodge-podge of APs with no controller and no management tools. It was not able to heal itself, and it was not able to handle the number of connections. In all the excitement, they had forgotten to plan for the new demand for wireless.

Implementing a wireless network requires a thoroughly thought-out design that will allow for flexibility, reliability, and resiliency in managing a saturated wireless network. In today's world, you need to understand the demand on your wireless network.

First, you have all the devices within your school that you know about (or think you know about): laptops, iPods, tablet devices, Android devices, Netbooks, Chromebooks, and so forth.

Second, you have your policy about employees and students bringing devices from home. If you allow devices to be brought in by employees and students, you need to plan for that. Most high school students these days have smartphones. Take for example a typical high school in California: 1,000 to 3,000 students, 150 or so faculty members, and 50 support positions, and everyone with a device that wants to connect to your wireless network!

Third, you have the wireless devices that will be carried onto your campus. Parents, UPS delivery folks, vendors, business partners, and volunteers all carry devices that will want to attach to your wireless network. Are you ready for that?

Building a wireless network that will support all of the devices that exist on your campus and those that will be brought onto your campus is not difficult. You can build a wireless network that will be safe for staff, kids, and parents to use (content filtered) and still protect your business assets. It is becoming quite common to segment wireless networks into four discrete segments: one for staff and teachers; another for students; another for guests (parents); and yet another for tech staff. Let's take a few minutes to discuss each one and why you want to have these wireless network segments (it's all about access to resources).

- Staff and teachers—This group of users will need access to business applications that students and the general public (guests) do not need, resources such as your student information system; finance; payroll; maintenance; human resources; and other services and resources like fileservers and printers that you want to keep secure from students and guests. This segment should be filtered for content.
- Students—This group will need access to resources that are important for their learning such as fileservers, network resources, printers, and applications that they use to support instruction. This segment should be filtered for content in support of your acceptable use policy. This group will not have access to any business applications.
- Guests—This group should have access only to the commercial Internet, and the access should be filtered for content (just like the student segment). This will provide guests secure access to the Internet but not allow them access to any corporate or student resources.

- Tech staff—This group needs access to everything in order to provide support across the organization.

Wireless Coverage vs. Saturation

There are two different models to consider when building a wireless infrastructure. One model is a wireless network that provides "coverage," and the other is a "saturated" wireless network.

Let's start with the coverage model. In this model you would survey your campus and all of the buildings that you want to use wireless devices in. What you are attempting to do is put in enough APs, at a certain distance apart, so that you can "roam" across the campus or through a building and not lose your connection to the network. Your concern is *not* how many devices you can connect at any given physical location, but that you can connect!

In this type of model you cannot ensure how many devices can connect at any given physical location. You and a few colleagues may be working in a classroom and your connection will be great. When thirty students walk into the room with wireless devices, the AP will become overwhelmed and will either start dropping connections or not allow new connections to become established. Imagine you are crossing a river in a rowboat. When two or three people are in the rowboat, the chances of them successfully crossing the river is pretty high. If thirty people all jump in the rowboat at once, the chances of a successful crossing are slim to none. The rowboat becomes overwhelmed and can't function effectively. Networks have a funny way of working wonderfully for the first few users and then crashing and burning once the whole school tries to connect. The same goes for wireless.

Think of a teacher who installs his or her own wireless AP to support some classroom laptops. That doesn't mean that each teacher can now do the same thing and the whole network will not grind to a halt—it will, guaranteed. And the cost to do the implementation correctly may be two to three times the expected cost because of the additional power, cabling, network equipment, and management hardware and software required for a campus-wide wireless network.

In a saturated wireless model, you would survey your campus and all of the buildings in a similar fashion; however, you are now taking into consideration *how many* devices can connect to the wireless network from any physical location. A saturated wireless network allows for many devices to connect to the wireless network and can support an influx of many new devices entering the same physical space.

In the coverage model, you can use fewer APs to build your network as well as ones that are less expensive to deploy. In a saturated wireless network, you need to use more APs and ones that have more intelligence. Access points in a saturated environment can detect when neighboring APs are under heavy demand, and they will auto adjust their antennas to support the additional demand and/or pass connections to a nearby AP that has spare capacity.

Building a saturated wireless environment costs more, but it is a wise investment. As we have discussed, the future is wireless, and there will only be more wireless devices entering your environment. Many IT practitioners now deploy one AP in every classroom to ensure a viable wireless network connection.

So how do you do all of this? It's not hard. It does take some time to get everything set up, but it is well worth the effort. If your IT needs support—this is one of those areas where you might want to use a consultant. You want to build it right the first time; if you do it incorrectly, you'll have to burn it to the ground and start again.

Building a saturated wireless network that will carry you into the future is a *Next* Practice.

ENTERPRISE COMPUTING AND THE DATA CENTER

When a school district recognizes the criticality of information systems is when the data center can become the center for enterprise computing. School districts have watched a cycle of centralization to decentralization then back again, similar to the private sector. First was the automation of student and financial information systems that drove district applications. Then the proliferation of classroom and lab computers and the local-area-network drove the client-server model. This model came with its own technological challenges, mainly that the distributed model was very complex to support and maintain. Additionally, wide-area network services couldn't provide the bandwidth to support centralized computing.

Today, wide-area network bandwidth is no longer the constraint in most areas. Virtualization—high-density servers and storage networks—require that information systems once again be centralized, both from an architectural standpoint, a cost standpoint, and a sustainability standpoint.

The effort should include the following initiatives.

Standardization of Technology-Based Curriculum and Computing Standards

Centralized computing and virtual desktop architectures will require the education technology department provide a list of standard applications that can then be licensed for centralized computing by the district. This will ensure

- Best opportunity for volume discounting—consolidating small separate purchase orders into one will warrant more discounting as well as better support for your organization's use of the software.
- Development of a scalable professional development model—a central-district resource can be assigned the task of developing a scalable professional development model. This will ensure not only some level of training and support but also a level of consistency in how the software is used throughout the school/district.
- High availability of application platforms—since virtualized applications are "Cloud-based," meaning that they are running in a virtual processor and storage platform, the probability of hardware failures is almost eliminated, except at the end-point.
- Centralized management of licenses—typically, when software is purchased by the site, there is no central record or administration of the software license. Many schools/districts practically ignore software licensing and pirate software openly. By centrally managing all district software licenses, the school/district can reliably state that they are in full compliance.
- Optimized support model for both information technology and education technology—the centralized support model works ideally with the centralized data center. Basically all technical resources are based and managed locally then dispatched to sites on an "as-needed" basis.

Design of High-Availability Computing Architectures

In a distributed environment—or truly a hybrid of centralized and distributed—the architecture for reliability is based on an uninterruptible power supply (UPS—a big battery) and a back-up appliance, or worse yet, tape. This model, although fundamentally correct, doesn't age well—meaning it gets dusty, the tapes get filled, and the batteries wear out. Spare hardware capable of running the district's critical applications are not kept on hand to provide a fail-safe platform. Because of these details, any failure brings about a site-wide shut-down.

Centralized core computing allows a single architecture for computing and storage to be maintained in an environmentally controlled and sustained envelope.

Consolidation of Computing and Storage Resources

Once a central data center is established, hardware can be consolidated and managed over a discrete, high-availability compute and storage platform. Individual arrays of disks at sites will no longer be required. Storage management software will allow all storage to be optimized and managed.

Virtualization of Applications and Services in Scale and Scope

Virtualization of operating systems will provide a platform immune to failure from hardware such as hard drives, interface cards, and motherboards.

Virtualization will allow scaling of compute power as necessary to support increases or decreases in application processing requirements—this is called "compute elasticity." For instance, if more computing power for the Student Information System (SIS) is required at the beginning of each quarter for increased adds/drops and SIS traffic, more compute processing cycles can be dedicated to this function—as needed to support the increased workflow—then reallocated to other functions when the increased processing power is no longer required.

Virtualization will also provide rapid deployment of new applications (expanded scope of applications), and development, through the use of virtual machines.

Eliminate Single Points-of-Failure

Once these platforms are established, the architecture is hardened by eliminating all single points-of-failure (SPOF). Obviously, most small-to medium-size school districts cannot afford to completely eliminate all SPOFs, but the process of identifying SPOFs, will allow the IT department to assess and prioritize mitigation activities and recovery processes.

The ultimate design would include secondary and/or even tertiary data centers, each data center separated by miles and in different power and network service regions. More on this later in the business continuity (BC) and disaster recovery (DR) section.

Developing an enterprise computing architecture in a data center is definitely a *Next* Practice.

VIRTUALIZATION

This could be the key to truly re-architect your data center computing platform, from facilities on up. But how can your district benefit from virtualization? You need a virtualization opportunity assessment.

First, what does it mean? Let's take it one word at a time. "Virtualization" is a centralized computing architecture that seeks to consolidate multiple hardware servers into a single, highly available (fault tolerant), and redundant computing architecture—usually multiple, quad-core servers and a storage area network (SAN). We've already discussed why consolidation is efficient and cost-effective.

What's a SAN? Think of it as a big chassis full of hard drives, with enough storage to run all of your district's server computing, and then a lot more. It also has redundant switches, called a "fabric," to create multiple high-speed paths between the servers and the storage.

The concept and philosophy of virtualization has been around since computing began sixty or so years ago—and always as applied to some specific technology—for example, memory, storage, and so forth. Today, it fundamentally is the disconnection between physical computing and the software running the computers—the ability to pool and optimize computing resources—sorry, I'm trying to keep it simple.

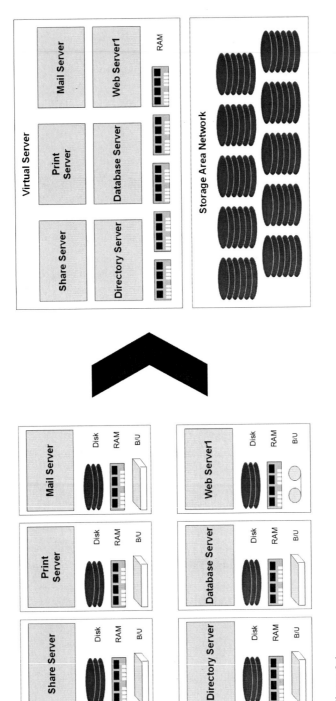

Figure 2.1.

Does it sound like putting all your computing eggs in one basket? In some ways it is, but the basket has so much fault tolerance and redundancy built into it that the likelihood of it completely failing is reduced to a manageable proportion. This is a true boon to your business continuity strategy. It won't, by the way, survive destruction of the building it resides in—thus your disaster recovery strategy applies.

Okay, back to the servers. Using a special new operating system called VMware (also Microsoft's HyperV), all the processing power in the "farm" of servers can be managed separately from the physical servers. So the typical virtualization exercise might consolidate 50 separate physical servers into 5 physical servers running 50 virtual servers. Each virtual server can have access to memory and storage as required for an application. So now, if your applications need more memory, you just allocate more memory to that application via the management software.

"Opportunity"—If your district's computing architecture has grown organically over a period of time, it probably has multiple servers dedicated to specific applications, each server with its own processors, memory, storage, operating system, applications, backup facility, and UPS. If this describes your data center (or lack of a data center, and you have servers sprawled all over your school sites), then you have a virtualization opportunity.

"Assessment"—If you have over twenty physical servers, you are a pretty good candidate for virtualization—the more servers, the better candidate. Of course, each school district is different. If your district has many servers at each site, then a robust wide-area-network (WAN) must be in place before you take on any consolidation or virtualization activities. But if you have a data center, with many dedicated servers, your opportunity is nigh. This is a perfect time to ask your technology department to compile a list of all of the applications and servers they support. This exercise will be an eye-opening experience for them and will give you a look at what is really out at the school sites.

Another main advantage of virtualization is portability. Portability refers to the ability to move virtual computing "instances" from one physical computing platform to another. I have to keep these descriptions somewhat vague because of the virtual-ness of it all—nothing in software is physically tied to hardware in the virtual space.

So what's next? How to begin? I tell my clients, "Before you spend another dollar on your computing architecture, review your business continuity and disaster recovery plans. If you don't have these, then you need to develop them—get help if you need it. This planning process will provide the basis for understanding and measuring the criticality, priority, size, and scale for your whole school/district information system."

Virtualization for purposes of increased performance, supportability, scalability, and recovery is a *Next* Practice.

DISASTER RECOVERY AND BUSINESS CONTINUITY

Disaster recovery (DR) and business continuity (BC) could be one of the most overlooked aspects of information technology planning and implementation.

Most small- to medium-size IT shops do their best to address DR via tape backup—which is fine as long as the solution is tested periodically and the required hardware/software is available in some form or fashion. However, as data center operations grow, the data center systems architecture needs to recognize the difference between BC and DR.

By definition, the foundation of BC is the standards, program development, and supporting policies—the guidelines and procedures needed to ensure an organization can continue without stoppage, irrespective of the adverse circumstances or events (http://en.wikipedia.org/wiki/Business_continuity).

Business continuity is in the context of eliminating single points-of-failure (SPOFs). In a high-availability design environment, each component in the computing, network, and storage areas is designed and implemented with layers of redundancy. The more critical your IT system is (I don't know of any school district that hasn't become totally dependent on its IT stuff), the more BC needs to be addressed.

Disaster recovery must be considered in the context of "What will we do if the district office burns down?" Any and all levels of BC can be rendered meaningless in the case of a disaster that destroys a whole building. For instance, if the building housing your data center were destroyed, what would be required to bring "critical" systems back online? SIS, e-mail, and transportation/Geographic Information System

(GIS) would need to be back online first. Is there a complete backup of data, applications software, and operating systems images that could be brought into production on some standard hardware? Is the original media available to create scratch operating-system builds? Are the operating-system build-procedures documented? Or is your hardware platform so customized that it couldn't be replicated no matter what? That really means that in a disaster, you couldn't come back up in weeks or even months.

To be clear, DR is a subset of BC. BC seeks to identify all likely points of failure and implement equipment, processes, and procedures to address each one.

Several BC components are implemented automatically as you plan your next server upgrade. For instance RAID (redundant array of independent disks) technology within your storage area network ensures that individual hard-drive failures won't affect BC by monitoring drive status, providing alerts in the event of failure, and allowing your IT guy to replace the drives using hot-swap technology.

Continue to address each potential SPOF through a top-down or bottom-up assessment. SAN switches are redundant to address switch fabric failure. Virtualization provides the ability (if implemented correctly) to move computing from one processor to another (VMotion). Core switches and servers are implemented with redundant power supplies to address power supply failure, and so forth.

For power, an uninterruptible power supply (UPS) allows minimal uptime in the case of power outage to keep servers running long enough for proper shut-down. This also means that the servers must be connected to the UPS to trigger this feature. An uninterruptible power supply without this feature only means a delayed failure. Also, remember that if your servers are running but your air conditioning isn't, your data center or server room will heat up at a rate equal to the number of servers and equipment in direct relation to the size of your server room. If temperatures climb over 110 degrees, equipment will not only be permanently damaged but will fail.

Take a systematic top-down or bottom-up approach and review each possible SPOF. Then address each according to its level of criticality. Obviously, this means an assessment of criticality comes first. Start with a BC and DR plan. Then create an implementation plan. Procure each component and implement with BC and DR in mind—you don't want your BC project to trigger your DR plan.

Verify BC and DR Practices

Finally, verification of BC and DR practices is rarely performed. We don't need to discuss why it isn't done—convenience, opportunity, downtime—but the risk of not planning and documenting a full recovery operation only ensures that when, or if, this disaster happens, the organization really doesn't know if the process and procedures will actually work. You can't know unless you test it—all of it.

Real disaster recovery and business continuity planning and implementation are a *Next* Practice.

CHAPTER 3

Planning for Education Technology Success — Curriculum Basis

CURRICULUM FOCUSED—PURPOSEFUL WORK

The most important factor to consider when planning a technology initiative is to start with the end in mind. Key questions to ask your planning team that everyone must be able to answer are

What is the curriculum focus of the district?
Is this project aligned and in support of our curriculum focus?
How is this going to impact instruction?
How will we measure the effectiveness of implementing a technology?

As simple as these questions are, we find that many school districts cannot answer them before starting an initiative, or they do not take the time to go through this process before starting on a curriculum initiative.

One of the most difficult things to do well is to focus on curriculum first and then decide which, if any, technologies support your curriculum efforts. When there is more than one curriculum initiative in your district, it is difficult to focus on one thing and do it well.

Dr. Holly McClurg, PhD, who is recognized as an expert in curriculum, talks about being *purposeful about our work*. Too often many initiatives fail due to lack of a *laser focus* on achieving a specific goal.

When there are too many initiatives within a school district, it is easy to lose focus, and it becomes difficult to measure the effectiveness of any technology initiative. By having a clearly defined laser focus on achieving a specific curriculum goal, it is much easier to implement technology to support that goal and measure the effectiveness in the use of a specific technology.

Before we examine some examples of technology initiatives, it is important to discuss the relationship between the assistant superintendent of curriculum and instruction and the director of technology. No other relationship is more important for the successful integration of technology. The job titles may be different as you look from district to district, however the function in all districts is the same: the cabinet-level person responsible for curriculum and instruction and the cabinet-level person responsible for technology (see figure 3.1). The success of integrating technology in support of curriculum lies specifically with these individuals.

It is not by accident that we define both of these positions as cabinet-level positions. Both curriculum and technology leaders in a school district need to be at the highest levels of the organization. If we expect technology to support instruction, then the technology side of the house has to be in sync with the curriculum side of the house. Clearly, communication and collaboration between the groups is essential, and their messages need to be shared with the entire cabinet.

A key factor for the success of any initiative is for the cabinet-level technologist to have a clear understanding of what educators want technology to do for them. (They really don't have to understand your job, but you need to understand theirs.) Technology leaders can very easily become too removed from the classroom. Their day gets consumed with technical issues, project management, politics, and e-mails.

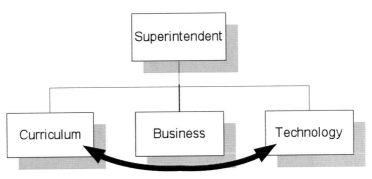

Figure 3.1.

Technology leaders should be spending about 20 percent of their time in classrooms!

Spending quality time in classrooms watching teachers in their craft and getting a deep understanding of what technologies might actually help students and teachers is a *Next* Practice.

When any curriculum or technology planning occurs in a school district, *both* of these leaders need to be present (or represented by senior technical staff).

Example

Over the past twenty years I have reviewed the technology implementations of a number of school districts. Some of the districts were quite large and others small. The process is quite simple. Before coming on site I ask the school district to provide for me a number of documents so that I can get a feel for what they are trying to accomplish and what their efforts to date have been. In every case I ask for them to document all of the applications that support instruction that are currently being used in the school district. Without fail they compile a *huge* list of applications that no one could have possibly imagined they were using! During one district review that I led, staff members were able to list over one hundred applications that were deployed at some level throughout the district. We all came together for a face-to-face meeting to discuss the findings. The team assembled was the superintendent, all of the cabinet members, a smattering of principals, the technology director and his staff, and an education technology teacher on special assignment. So I began to ask my questions.

"Who owns these applications from a business or instructional sense?"
(Crickets . . .)
"Who is evaluating the effectiveness of these applications?"
(More crickets . . .)
"How do these applications support the curriculum goals of the district?"
(Now it's getting uncomfortable.)
"What are the curriculum goals of the district?"

(Somebody pulls out a binder and says, "We have curriculum goals."
Whew!)

These are questions everyone at the executive level should be asking themselves and their staff. Without a laser-focus approach to curriculum initiatives and the technology that supports them, failure is
imminent.

So my questions continued.

"OK, we can all see that we have way too many applications that we
are trying to support in this school district, so let's start getting rid
of them. I think we should get rid of Read 180 what do you think?"
Response from the team: "You can't do that. We use that application
every day."
My response: "How do you know it is effective? Who has evaluated
this application?"
(More silence . . . time to let them off the hook . . . they get the message.)

Using any technology because it feels good, or because the vendor
said it would help students achieve, is not a justification for implementation. Unless someone takes ownership of technology use and the
applications, you are doomed and will fail.

Example

*Technology for the Sake of Technology: A Solution Looking
for a Problem*

This is not an uncommon phenomenon. Many school districts have
technology directors who are very excited when new technologies
come out. As mentioned before, one school district deployed over
1,000 iPads to students without any sense of how they were going to
support the devices (our opinion). How were they going to manage the
syncing of the devices? How did this particular device support their
current curriculum efforts?—It didn't! But it was a really cool new
technology that is very popular in the consumer market. They did shift

their curriculum focus to fit the device, however, because they found out that the applications they were using for their initial curriculum focus did not work on the new iPads.

The focus on curriculum must come first, and it requires strong leadership and direction from the superintendent and the most senior cabinet members for any technology initiative to be successful.

Strong curriculum focus that is supported by senior leadership is a *Next* Practice.

PROFESSIONAL DEVELOPMENT—YOUR DISTRICT'S PRIORITIES, PRACTICES, AND REALITIES

An imperative for any technology initiative to be successful is professional development. Just as we profess to be purposeful about our work and to have a laser focus on achieving curriculum goals, we must have the same focus and commitment in providing professional development.

Professional development should be in support of your curriculum goals. Ask yourself the same questions about professional development that you should ask about technology.

Who owns this professional development activity?
How will we measure its effectiveness?
How does this support the curriculum goals of the district?

Example

In a recent deployment of technology in a fifth-grade classroom to support our focus on writing, I allocated forty hours of professional development for the teacher. The deployment consisted of integrating laptop computers for every student in the class in support of the curriculum goal. The first six hours of the professional development consisted of the teacher getting to know and understand the technology that was going to be deployed in her classroom. Classroom management techniques, logistics, and care and feeding of the technology were the focus. The remaining thirty-four hours were spent on planning out the next trimester by examining her course of study and determining the best opportunities to integrate technology. Professional development should focus the majority of time on curriculum and not just on the technology. Without providing teachers with the skills to integrate the technology, the technology will fail in its primary mission of supporting curriculum goals.

Earlier we discussed the importance of the relationship between the assistant superintendent of curriculum and instruction and the director of technology. Once again you can see how imperative it is that these leaders in your school district work, communicate, and collaborate to ensure a successful integration of technology. It is ultimately the responsibility of these two leaders to ensure that professional development is in alignment with the curriculum goals and the technology initiatives in support of those curriculum efforts.

Another factor to consider when implementing technology in support of curriculum is the professional development required for your technical staff. Many times this is a group that is forgotten. The technical staff needs to be brought in early on with any technology initiative. They have a unique way of looking at technology initiatives and may need training or support in order to support the project. Perhaps there is new server or backend hardware that will have to be implemented. Reporting tools or technical methods deployed to support the technology must also be supported. Many times this will require the technical staff to obtain professional development from a technical source. Technical schools can be very expensive (but you get what you pay for) and should be budgeted for in your planning. It is not uncommon to spend $3,000 to $5,000 for a week of technical training.

Professional development is the key Next Practice *that supports the true scope and scale of technology impact in the classroom.*

TECHNOLOGY PLANNING VERSUS IMPLEMENTATION PLANNING

Without a technology plan, chaos will be the order of the day. Precious resources will be wasted, and in the end the impact on instruction will be minimal and unmeasurable. How can you determine what to buy if you haven't determined what you will do with a particular technology?

Many schools and districts, with the help of parent organizations or donors, purchase classroom devices without determining what or how they will be used; the devices may be really cool or the latest gadget to cruise the Internet, but how do they support the curriculum efforts of the district? These purchases are rarely reviewed and/or approved by the IT department. If this is happening in your district, we can assume that you have no plan for technology, or technology standards.

This chapter will discuss how to take the subjective planning process over the implementation hump.

Oftentimes a conversation between Education Technology and IT goes like this.

Education Technology—*We need thirty-two laptops in Mr. X's classroom.*

IT—*What will you use them for?*

Education Technology—*We will be piloting our one-to-one project.*

IT—*What will you do with them?*

Educational Technology—*The students will use them.*

IT—*What will the students do with them?*

Educational Technology—*They will use them in the classroom for their projects.*

IT—*What software will they be using?*

Educational Technology—*Software X.*

IT—*Is it paid for?*

Educational Technology—*They already have a copy.*

IT—*Really? Will it work with the new laptops?*

The questions that still haven't been asked will be

How will the new laptops be networked?
Do they need printers?
Where will they be stored?
How will they be charged?
Who will be responsible to secure them?
Who will support them when there is a technical issue?
Who will support them when there is a software issue?

The key to progress beyond this exercise requires four things: a curriculum plan, a technology plan, an infrastructure plan, and a budget plan.

The curriculum plan obviously is not a technology plan and must be endorsed by leadership and defined by the teaching staff.

The technology plan defines the technologies required to support the curriculum plan. This plan will identify the software requirements, hardware requirements, implementation, and professional development plans.

The infrastructure plan details the underlying facilities and technology required. For instance, a curriculum plan that requires wireless devices may trigger a network equipment upgrade that triggers a facilities upgrade, such as building modifications or power upgrades. The infrastructure plan should be detailed enough to procure specific equipment, services, and software, and to define implementation resources and timelines.

The budget plan should be detailed enough to provide a rough order of magnitude estimate and the basis for procurement. The budget plan should include:

- Hardware
- Software (licenses)
- Installation services
- Configuration services
- Maintenance services

And ongoing or recurring costs.

The Trouble with the Technology Plan

Many schools/districts develop a technology plan that looks something like this:

By 2013, 20 percent of our classrooms will have electronic learning resources.

By 2014, 40 percent of our classrooms will have electronic learning resources.

In 2013, 20 percent of our teachers demonstrate competency using 21st-century learning goals.

Blah, blah, blah.

The trouble with these types of technology plans is that they provide a lot of detail about what results are preferred, but rarely do they address actual infrastructure, equipment, and hard budgets to achieve the goals or the process of how to achieve the goals.

The education technologist needs to interpret the desired outcomes presented in the technology plan and then needs to work with the information technology department to determine what infrastructure will be required to achieve the outcomes. Oftentimes the budgets developed by the instructional side of the house don't provide a realistic estimate for the infrastructure that will be required—mainly because there is a fundamental lack of depth of understanding of infrastructure requirements for campus-wide and/or district-wide technology implementations.

Technology Leadership

Technology strategy starts at the top—really. This doesn't mean that the superintendent must write the plan. It means that the plan must be

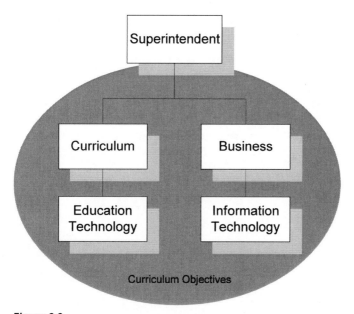

Figure 3.2.

developed, endorsed, and communicated from the top down. Although the superintendent as well as the board of education typically sign off on district "technology plans," they rarely are more than check-off approvals. However, technology *strategy* must be established at the cabinet level, otherwise, when it comes time to ask for resources, everything will come into question. At all costs, the following two questions must be anticipated, answered, and most importantly during a board meeting, avoided: "Why are we doing that?" and "Who made that decision?" By the time a plan or procurement reaches the board, it should be communicated and fully vetted by information technology, educational technology, and each name up the ladder.

Executive sponsorship of technology initiatives is critical in that district- or enterprise-wide implementations must be based on strategy and standards. These strategies and standards must be embraced at the highest level, otherwise, the commitment and funding opportunities will be subject to the most finicky board member's mood on that late-evening board action.

The process of developing and establishing a technology strategy, one that starts and ends with district leadership, is a *Next* Practice.

CHAPTER 4

The Way Forward

THE STRATEGIC PLANNING PROCESS

To get started, a formal strategic planning process should be under-taken, sponsored at the highest level, and performed by someone ob-jective and beyond the reach of departmental politics. I'm trying not to say, Use a consultant, but . . . yes, use a consultant.

The discovery process—including the kick-off meeting—should in-clude stakeholders at the highest level as possible in order to establish objectives and set expectations. The former is obvious, the latter is less so. Board members, the superintendent, the cabinet, education technol-ogy leaders, information technology leaders, and principals must be included in the strategic-planning process.

The discovery process is used not only as an opportunity to gather, compile, and analyze information; it is also an opportunity to gain buy-in and build credibility of the methodology and expected outcomes and deliverables.

By forcing departments to come together, share information, and agree upon objectives, the process gains validity and credibility, while a process lacking these fundamental processes is doomed to fail.

The primary objective of the discovery process is to identify and gain consensus on the district mission, goals, and objectives in support of curriculum and technology goals.

If the technologist can summarize the objectives in a two-to-four-bullet list, the primary agenda of the kick-off has been accomplished and needs to be communicated throughout the organization. If this cannot be attained, then it will need to be developed and accepted before further research or planning can proceed. Any work performed, assumptions made, or designs established would be made without executive sponsorship, and suddenly those questions would come up again—What are we doing? Who made that decision?

The most destructive comments that can come after the fact are

- I don't know how they came up with that.
- I didn't make that decision.
- They didn't ask me about that.

Once goals and objectives are established, it will be contingent on the four key groups (three in a small district) to lay the groundwork for the rest of the process.

1. The curriculum group must develop curriculum needs and requirements.
2. The education technology group must develop system needs and requirements.

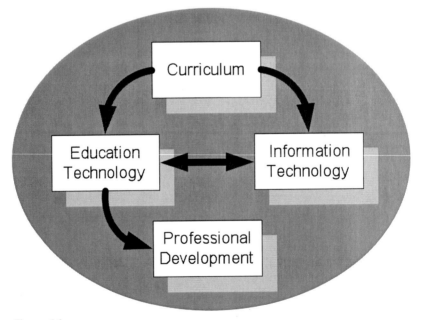

Figure 4.1.

3. The information technology group must develop technical needs and requirements.

4. The professional development group must develop the training, communication, and follow-up plans.

STRATEGY VERSUS TACTICS

Example

Imagine it is the 1800s and you are planning a long journey to a far away land. Your goals and objectives will dictate what you are trying to accomplish and why. You will have to determine, in general, where you would like to end up, and what you will need when you get there. For instance, if you were in St. Louis, and you had to travel west, your objective might be to live in San Francisco.

Your strategy will be the general ways and means to accomplish your objectives. In this example, you would decide that the best way would be to join a wagon-train headed west.

Your tactics are what you need to execute your strategy. How will you travel? What path and when? What supplies will you need during the journey? Even, how will you navigate and measure your progress?

Your tactics would be to buy some oxen and a covered-wagon, supplies, rations, hunting rifles and ammunition, etc.

These strategic and tactical plans are just as important as the vision itself. Where the vision provides the ultimate goal, the development of the strategy and tactics will give you the first indication of whether this goal can be achieved or not. Do the paths and methods even exist?

As you lay down the tactical requirements, you will gain understanding for the investment in time and resources necessary to make the journey.

Developing a Strategy

Once you have developed and communicated clear goals and objectives, you can develop a strategy that will address *how* to accomplish the goals and objectives. It is actually an iterative process starting from goals and objectives, identifying a strategic component, and then circling around to see how this strategic component impacts the stated goals and objectives. If that component doesn't fully address the objective, then there may be multiple strategic initiatives to address each objective. For instance, a wireless implementation may require more than just adding wireless APs. It may involve upgrading or acquiring other components to complete the network upgrade. Therefore, your objective statements may include the need to upgrade network infrastructure in addition to adding wireless antennae.

Then you would need to identify a number of strategies to achieve your objective.

In the business world, we utilize a formal planning process (see figure 4.2).

The main phases of the process are

1. Needs identification
2. Needs analysis/assessment
3. Preliminary recommendations
4. A feasibility study
5. A design and implementation plan

The process may go like this.

Let's assume that Education Technology has researched and determined which math software best will align with the district's curriculum objectives. They have decided that they will implement a standardized math curriculum suite in all secondary schools.

That is now the objective—one assumes that somehow they know that this math curriculum will achieve their ultimate academic goals. As technologists, we just build it, without questioning it. So if this math-curriculum software requires each student have a device, then, suddenly, we have a one-to-one math initiative.

Samples of Objectives, Strategies, and Tactics

Objective: Each student will use standard math curriculum software in the classroom.

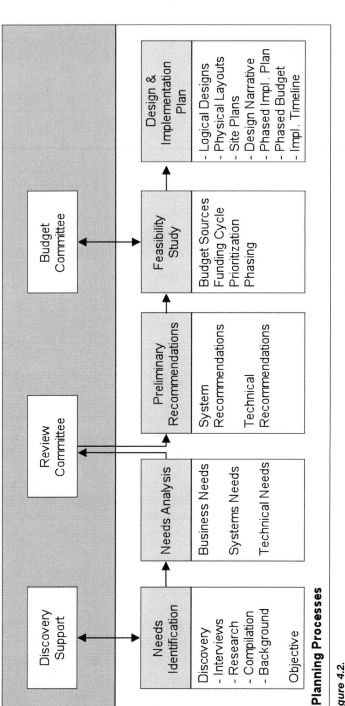

Planning Processes

Figure 4.2.

Strategy:

1. Identify standardized math curriculum software
2. Build wireless networking infrastructure
   a. Upgrade cabling
   b. Upgrade network equipment
   c. Manage wireless networking
3. Build data center
   a. Upgrade WAN
   b. Manage internal Cloud hosts
   c. Establish business continuity and disaster recovery
4. Implement technology classrooms
   a. Procure equipment
   b. Establish professional development
   c. Roll out
5. License curriculum software
   a. Establish professional development
   b. Roll out

Tactics: The tactics for this example project would immediately begin to get very detailed. Suffice it to say that item 2, Build wireless networking infrastructure, would be broken down into several tasks and projects, each with its own technical design and budget.

DEVELOPMENT OF THE TECHNOLOGY PLAN

Development of any plan requires a level of formality. There are many reasons why technology plans never come to fruition. IT director–level people typically

1. Have had no formal strategic planning or project management training;
2. Are simply too busy managing day-to-day operations to spend time developing a formal document;
3. Don't have a platform to present a strategic plan (meaning that in the course of their employment, they have not been asked to present a formal plan, and thus have never done one). Remember

when we discussed the placement of the technology department in the organization? And that it needs to be placed at the cabinet level? This will help remove excuses for not developing a plan and making your technology department strategic to your district.

This ignores the fact that there is often a specific technology planning requirement for many schools. However, these "technology plans" typically call for data and planning developed on the instructional side of the house with only minor involvement of IT in order to comply with some standard requirement or to gain access to grant funds. The problem is these plans aren't written from a technical design and procurement standpoint. They lay out the vision and expected outcomes of the plan, but they don't detail the necessary steps to get there. Nor do they typically provide technical specifications, designs, and detailed budgetary information needed to bring these plans to fruition. The issue is not that this level of detail is necessary for the purposes of these plans, it's that the actual implementation plans are never sanctioned and developed.

To address this "need to plan" in the present tense, an awareness of significant "need" must be urgent enough to warrant action from leadership. What does that mean? You sometimes need a crisis. Something needs to happen to cause school/district leadership to request, sponsor, and support (pay for) the strategic-planning process. Or with strong leadership at the superintendent level, you can motivate your cabinet into action.

In the technology world, typically, the building of new buildings, a bond being passed, investment in new technology initiatives, or the failure of the existing technology infrastructure is a crisis opportunity. Whatever the case, this opportunity must be taken to its fullest potential, or you risk constant failure and chronic system underperformance.

As consultants, we typically get brought in with the luxury of executive sponsorship and a defined scope of work. The following is an abridged version of a formal planning process that works particularly well for IT and education technology scopes, and it can be used as an outline to develop any medium-scale and/or medium-scope IT project.

Needs Identification
Discovery
- Interviews
- Research
- Compilation
- Background
Objectives

Figure 4.3.

Needs Identification and Objectives

The first task is to identify the stakeholders and get them together to agree on the goals of the initiative. Projects of large scale and scope may indeed need a mission statement.

The objectives should be broadly stated, nonspecific, and incontrovertible. Objectives should be summarized in two to four bullet points even though their implications may be far reaching.

For instance, if your school wants to become wireless, your objective would be "Provide mobile computing to all students in all classrooms." This doesn't address the fact that the fiber backbone and core switching needs to be upgraded to support this—these facts will come out in the next process, the needs analysis.

In formalized planning, the objectives come from an in-depth needs-identification process. This is a deep-dive into what the team thinks they have, where they are now, and where they think they are going. The process starts with a kick-off meeting that should accomplish the following:

- Identify stakeholders and convene them on the basis of this initiative
- Identify key resources who may not be present
- Set expectations of milestones, timelines, and deliverables

Additional data collection will be required by all departmental stakeholders—these are not just the department heads. This requires separate meetings with the departmental staff in an effort to gain input from any party who may have an interest or a concern.

It is critical at this early stage to develop credibility among all participants that the process will yield results. Whether or not the results meet their individual satisfaction is not necessarily the goal. The goal is primarily to ask for input, to provide the opportunity to discuss proposed objectives and expected results, and to propose general timetables. Everyone must have an opportunity to affect the process.

Not gaining credibility will ensure there will be naysayers in your midst.

Needs Analysis

The needs-analysis process seeks to identify the requirements necessary to achieve the objectives. The requirements can be categorized granularly as follows: business needs, systems needs, and technical needs. Keep in mind that these "needs" are still on the requirements side of the planning process, as opposed to the solution side of the process. We are still not ready to design or plan anything yet.

Needs Analysis
Business Needs
Systems Needs
Technical Needs

Figure 4.4.

Business needs are the needs as described by the business requirements. Typically this does not include specifics about a hardware or software solution—those are systems needs. The business needs should be descriptive regarding the business model and how this project intends to affect it positively.

In education, business needs are the curriculum requirements.

Systems needs are the needs as described by the systems requirements. It may name software systems or hardware architectures, but it might not name actual technologies or products.

Technical needs are needs detailed and specified by technology, scope, and scale. The technical needs are specific enough to be turned into a requirements definition of a request for proposal (RFP), or possible technical specifications. Technical needs support procurement—but wait, we can't buy anything yet.

Example

The following is an example of the needs analysis for a one-to-one curriculum project based on a hypothetical instructional software called Xware. The software has been identified as supporting the curricular goals for high school math. Xware software is a Cloud-based software service. The Xware software was actually picked in response to identified curriculum (business) needs.

The curriculum needs for this project are as follows:

- The high school math department is committed to implementing common core standards.
- The high school's students must have interactive tools for learning math according to 21st-century learning models.
- The high school math department has determined that Xware software supports all math curriculum objectives and common core standards.

The systems needs for this project are the following:

- Xware is a software-based instructional application that teacher and student interact with in real-time, doing classroom exercises as well as collecting progress data and student assessments.
- Xware software must be licensed for the teacher and each student computer.
- The teacher and each student must have access to a computer during class.
- The teacher will require training and coaching for Xware software.
- The teacher and students will require study materials.

The technical needs for this project are as follows:

- Xware software is Cloud-based, therefore each teacher and student computer must have access to the school/district wireless or wired network and Internet access.
- Xware software is Windows-based, therefore each teacher and student computer must be Windows-based or running a virtual Windows desktop (thin-client).
- The classroom must support thirty-three wireless computers.
- Every secondary math classroom must support thirty-three wireless computers.
- Every classroom in secondary campuses could be a math class, therefore every classroom must be able to support thirty-three wireless computers.
- The wireless network must support virtual local area network (VLAN) segmentation for student access to instructional software.
- The site LAN must have provision to support thirty-three computers in each supported classroom.
- The district WAN must have provision to support the projected bandwidth requirements of Xware along with all other applications at the core.
- The district Internet connection must be provisioned for projected user requirements for Xware and all other Internet-based applications.

As you can see from the above examples, the business needs are general- and objective-oriented, while the systems needs begin to describe the proposed solution at the system level. The technical needs are the specific equipment, software, and services required to take the next formal step.

Before beginning the next step in our planning process—preliminary recommendations—it is imperative to review the needs analysis with the project stakeholders. Each statement in the plan, from objective through technical needs, should be clearly stated, and undebatable. If consensus is not found in the review process, then the needs must be adjusted and/or compromised to ensure buy-in by stakeholders before moving to the next step. If this acknowledgement is not gained, you can be sure that later on in the process, that person will say, "I didn't agree to that." To mitigate these objections, a well-thought-out needs analysis and point-by-point review should address all objections.

It should be noted that there may be some who will never agree to some specific objective or detail. It will be the responsibility of the planner to identify, document, and communicate this standing objection, and to maximize support at the higher levels. If the dissension is at the leadership level, the plan will have to change.

Preliminary Recommendations
System Recommendations
Technical Recommendations

Figure 4.5.

Finally, to cement these acknowledgements, a formal document should be delivered fully detailing the discovery process and the results (objectives and needs analysis). This *draft* document should be circulated and approved by departmental heads and stakeholders. If warranted, a formal sign-off document should be attached and signatures obtained from stakeholders and leadership. Sometimes this is necessary in order to protect your plan from future attacks.

Preliminary Recommendations

You may wonder why the next step is called *Preliminary* Recommendations. Why include a step that is intentionally incomplete? Well, for lack of a better name, this step might also be called Blue Sky Solution, or Dream Big/Dream On.

The result of this step is to develop the "best" solution to address the needs identified, not necessarily the cheapest, or even a cost-effective, solution. This step can only be preliminary because we don't have a method to control the scope, scale, and priorities of the proposed solution set.

What that means is that all we can hope to design at this point is a Blue Sky solution, or the "ultimate" solution available. This is actually the step where many consultants leave their clients hanging. The "best" solution rarely is the final solution because it doesn't take into account the fiscal environment, as well as other external factors that may, in the end, dictate all or significant parts of the solution set.

Yet this step cannot be skipped as it is critical to establish the metrics for project success—or achievement of objectives. The exercise involves designing the ultimate solution—the way it would be done if money were no object—and then again, confirming with stakeholders that the solution addresses all needs and achieves all objectives.

The preliminary recommendations will provide the concept and design guidelines for the proposed solution. The recommendations may be detailed enough to identify products and architectures but not necessarily a complete implementation cost model.

The purpose of this step is, once again, to gain consensus from stakeholders that the "preliminary" proposed solution set will achieve the original stated objectives. If the "blue sky" solution set doesn't gain credence with the stakeholders, what are the chances that a scoped-down or scaled-back solution will?

If for some reason, at this early stage, all objectives cannot be accomplished, or at least addressed, then the expectations will be set with the stakeholders that the final solution *will not* achieve all stated goals. This may warrant a revision to the objectives, or the needs, and perhaps prioritizing and addressing them at a later date.

The preliminary recommendations should provide complete solutions regarding systems and platforms, as well as technical recommendations which should include technologies, products (manufacturers), and architectures. The preliminary recommendations would not at this stage include a bill of materials (BOM), which details budget estimates or detailed implementation schedules.

All stakeholders should have the opportunity to review the preliminary recommendations and object to them or discuss them to their satisfaction. This process will ensure continued buy-in and support as the next critical phases come along. Even if all the stakeholders don't completely agree with all the recommendations, they will at least understand all the relevant considerations.

Feasibility Study

Feasibility is the process of determining if the *fiscal* and *physical* environment will support the preliminary recommendations. If not, then adjustments to project scope, scale, and scheduling will come into play. Many other factors can come into play in a feasibility study, but for IT projects specifically, economic feasibility and system feasibility are the most relevant.

Feasibility includes a review not only of fiscal opportunity (economic feasibility), but also of practical potential (system feasibility). For instance, if the district is considering a network upgrade at a site, they will not only need to review the cost of the network upgrade but also the cost and practicality of all the other systems impacted by the upgrade, such as facilities, power, and structured cabling. What impact will this upgrade have on the rest of the schools, or on district standards?

It is important to note that the technologist must recognize that a network equipment upgrade will require facilities, structured cabling, and power infrastructure—and the last two systems could easily outweigh the cost of the network equipment.

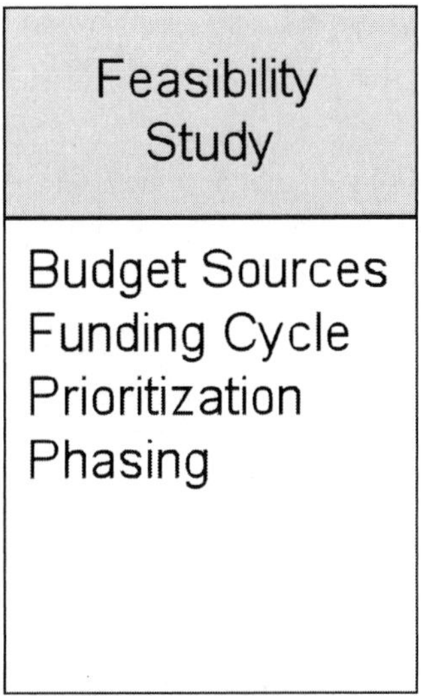

The feasibility study involves an understanding of the current and future availability of funds, as well as any restrictions on the use of funds. For instance, in a three-year modernization program, it would be important to understand the amount of funding available for each year. Since infrastructure components would need to be installed before computing devices, the investments would not necessarily track evenly year-to-year. Additionally, some bond programs don't allow end-user devices

Feasibility Study

Budget Sources
Funding Cycle
Prioritization
Phasing

Figure 4.6.

to be purchased with bond funds. These considerations require that the district have other discretionary or matching funding that must be available at the necessary time to complete a project.

Although the technologist may not be privy to all the budgetary information, the more data available, the more detailed and effective the cost modeling.

The process of the feasibility study involves a review of the preliminary recommendations, a rough order of magnitude cost estimate, and information regarding funding and the funding cycle.

An initial gap analysis between the rough order of magnitude cost estimate and the funding information will provide the metric for scope, scale, and prioritization.

At this point, a detailed cost model should be established. This cost model should allocate budget, and contingency, for every aspect of the project, from infrastructure through commissioning and professional development. All costs should be modeled based on industry standards for materials, labor, taxes, shipping, maintenance contracts, training, and on-going support services. Professional development budgets should also be addressed, including substitutes, materials, and in-service costs.

All recurring costs should be annualized and budgeted for the life-cycle of the implementation and beyond. These recurring costs must be analyzed for budget compliance. Some bond language may not allow funding for such things as maintenance contracts or on-going services.

Implementation planning needs to be based on the availability of funds. For instance, if the implementation plan calls for structured cabling upgrades of $1 million in year 1, then that $1 million must exist in a budget somewhere, or the Chief Business Officer needs to advise the technologist of the actual funds available.

The Design and Implementation Plan

The design and implementation plan is the heart of the tactical plan. The design and implementation plan will examine each point in the tactical plan, and detail the how and when for each building-block of the tactical plan.

Design & Implementation Plan
- Logical Designs - Physical Layouts - Site Plans - Design Narrative - Phased Impl . Plan - Phased Budget - Impl . Timeline

Figure 4.7.

Example

The strategic plan may state, "Implement campus-wide wireless in all secondary sites."

The tactical plan may state, "Install 35 wireless access points (WAPs), wireless controller, and configure them to work under the district Wireless Management Suite."

The design and implementation plan would provide timing, sequencing, and an identified budget.

The design and implementation plan would include the following components.

Design

Typically this requires a diagram and narrative detailing the specific equipment (hardware and software), architecture, and configuration details that can be used to build an actual bill of materials (BOM) for use in a procurement vehicle such as a request for quote (RFQ) or request for proposal (RFP). The design may include the following:

- Single-line diagrams detailing the equipment and their wired connections
- Logical designs detailing the arrangement of equipment as related to infrastructure and other interdependent systems (such as the relation between network switches and WAN routers)
- Scaled drawings that detail the location of items within a room or rack where specific physical installation requirements exist
- Site plans that provide locations of equipment or infrastructure within the site (such as IDF and MDF locations or WAP locations)

Budget

The budget, or cost model, may be the most significant part of the tactical plan. All budgets are estimates, therefore they are evaluated not for accuracy, but for vision. Think about the first budget project you developed, and how much you overlooked.

Although a budget never consists of just equipment (hardware/software), that is typically the starting point. This will be repeated throughout this section, but using the OSI model is a good way to help build a comprehensive budget. Open Systems Interconnection (OSI) is an effort to standardize computer networking that was started in 1977 by the International Organization for Standardization (ISO), along with the ITU-T. For example, if you are developing a network upgrade budget, start with the network equipment plus taxes and shipping (forgetting these can immediately throw your estimate off by 10–15 percent). Next estimate the cost of all the accessories and related equipment, such as cables and UPSs. Then include maintenance contracts and other recurring costs. Also include installation, and configuration services. Add training and knowledge transfer for the support staff. Finally, address professional development costs.

From there, you would move up and down the OSI model to identify all systems and infrastructure impacted by the network upgrade.

A complete description of building a cost model would be too detailed for the objective of this book, but suffice it to say that each item should include hard costs, taxes, shipping, installation/implementation services, maintenance contracts, and contingency.

The amount of the contingency for each component must be developed based on some past experience or standard. Any technologist will approach each estimated cost from more than one angle in order to qualify each cost. For instance, for estimating a structured cabling project, the technologist may use a per-drop industry standard for one estimate, then take a materials-and-labor cost for the second estimate. The greater of the two, with some contingency, might then be selected.

The Implementation Plan and Timeline

The implementation plan may take the form of many formatted reports, including, but not limited to

- bulleted lists,
- Gantt charts,
- a project plan (Microsoft Project),
- a critical path analysis.

Developing a formal design and implementation plan is a *Next* Practice.

DEVELOP TECHNOLOGY STANDARDS
(PRACTICES AREN'T STANDARDS)

Just because you've "always done it that way" doesn't mean it is a standard. Oftentimes in organizations, as a consultant I can ask, "Why is it done that way?" And the answer often times is "We've always done it that way, even though . . . that person isn't here anymore."

Invariably, better, more efficient processes and systems can improve legacy processes and systems. However, there must be the impetus to seek change and improvement.

It is important for a *Next* Practices organization to *establish standards for technology and to communicate effectively throughout the organization what the standards are and how they came to be.* The best way to enforce standards is through the procurement process. If they can't buy it, then your standards will remain intact.

Anytime I see hardcopy paperwork, I ask, "Can't this be done electronically?" Often the answer is yes. The trick is to be in a position to challenge the status quo and be able to offer viable solutions.

This doesn't mean that practices can't become standards. This is typical of the "pilot project" or "proof-of-concept." There is no existing standard, so we should do a pilot project. Based on the outcomes, the pilot project will be revised or improved, and it will then become the standard.

Don't get caught, however, in the pilot-project trap. There are many issues that arise from pilot projects that don't get solved, and thereby, no standards are developed and no broader initiative or standard results.

Many schools and districts can point to technology installations that were pilot projects, but nothing became of them. Now the pilot program is more like a technology island.

Or worse, your school might have multiple technology "pilot" projects, all unrelated and run by different people, with no real intent to develop a district-wide standard. These installations are a total waste of time, money, and effort, and at best they may positively impact only a select few students.

All technology "pilot" projects must be sanctioned by Information Technology and Educational Technology, and they must be evaluated as a potential for standardization. If there is no long-range budget to support a district-wide implementation, then what is the purpose of the "pilot"?

Technology Standards—The Sniff Test

We'll discuss the development of technology standards in more detail in the enterprise management section, but it is important to address the question of what should be standardized and what shouldn't.

Standards should be developed for technology-based curriculum initiatives that will affect

- all schools,
- all of a selection of grade levels across schools,
- or all of a discipline across schools.

Here are some of the considerations involved.

Enterprise-Wide

If the initiative, or project, is not enterprise-wide, then it likely doesn't warrant a standard. For instance, if your high school journalism class decides to implement newspaper publishing software, the potential overall impact is only on other journalism classes. This doesn't justify creating a district-wide standard.

However, if your district has two hundred schools, and the district could purchase a site-license for every school at a significant discount, then a standard would be justified.

District Budget

Without specific funding, there is no need to develop a district standard. It's hard to say, "You can't buy that, even though I'm not paying for it."

If the district sees that all elementary math classes are purchasing a variety of math curriculum software, this might merit creating a district standard. This is why centralization of technology and technology resources is so essential.

Obviously, system support and sustainability will become an issue as a variety of specialty software programs proliferate within the district.

The district may decide to encourage cooperation between the sites, pool the site funds, and seek volume discounts or site licenses. Professional development can then support optimal and standardized use of the standardized software.

Equity Considerations

Sometimes a limited budget brings out the worst in a school district. Technology strategy must address equity, or risk being a pet project.

If a district standard cannot benefit *all* teachers and students, then the justification and reasoning must pass muster with the have-nots.

For example, in one project, it was determined that all the math and science classrooms in secondary schools were to receive classroom technology upgrades as the result of a bond initiative. The first part of the dilemma was addressed in the bond language, which called for technology for math and science. However, the it's-not-the-teacher's-classroom issue came up immediately (more on this issue later).

Later it became clear that the principals were maneuvering teachers and manipulating classroom assignments in an attempt to maximize the number of classrooms that were upgraded. In the end, several history teachers were using math classrooms to the dismay of other non-math teachers.

Controversial Initiatives

Sometimes the process of developing a standard reveals that no standard is better—or more acceptable to the masses.

If an initiative is controversial at the outset, the likelihood of standardization success is diminished by the ability to get buy-in from all stakeholders.

This is the "choose-your-battles-wisely" recommendation. The Macintosh versus PC argument has left many casualties. It only takes one board member to impale you with all your logical arguments to move to a single platform—in spectacular fashion and in front of live audiences often.

Developing and enforcing technology standards is a *Next* Practice.

BE CAREFUL NOT TO TAKE TOO LONG OF A VIEW

One of the driving factors for technology implementation in education is bond modernization programs. Although these programs are a boon to technology upgrades, it forces technologists to attempt to create long-range plans that have a longer time horizon than many technology platforms—while buildings are built to last fifty years, technology can't be planned more than five years out. Even this horizon is a little too long for some technologies.

The technology lifecycle must be taken as a key consideration for bond-financed investments. Is it appropriate to spend bond money, financed with taxpayer money as a 15-to-30-year debt, on device technology with a two-year lifecycle?

Technology investments should be divided into their lifecycles and planned obsolescence. Infrastructure and core equipment will have longer lifecycles and are appropriate for long-term investment. User devices and classroom technologies have shorter lifecycles and should be considered possibly inappropriate for bond investments.

Figure 4.8 gives some practical lifecycle expectations for technology.

Technology	Description	Lifecycle
End-points	Laptops, Computers, Tablets	2-3 years
Classroom Equipment	Amplifiers, Document Cameras, DVD Players, Projectors	3-5 years
Network Equipment	Edge Switches, WAPs, UPSs	3-5 years
Core Equipment	Core Switches, Routers, Filters, SANs, DR devices	4-8 years
Infrastructure	Fiber Backbones, Copper Horizontal, IDFs, MDFs, Environmental	7-15 years

Figure 4.8.

Classroom Technology Standards—The Classroom Doesn't Belong to the Teacher, It Belongs to the School District (Shhhh . . . Don't Tell Them!)

In a recent meeting I had with a district education-technology coordinator, the subject of printers came up. Before tackling the pros and cons of laser versus color versus networked, the education-technology coordinator spoke first, saying, "Don't talk with the teachers."

The classroom doesn't belong to the teacher. If standards are created for classrooms, exceptions should not be made for specific teachers—the standards would no longer be standards then.

We don't mean *never* talk with the teachers. Obviously they are the ones (and the students) we are most trying to impact. In fact, in other areas of this book, we emphasize the need to talk with the teachers.

What we mean in this instance is that technology standards should be based on a formal assessment and inquiry—individual technology components should be procured based on established standards.

It is difficult enough to develop technology standards for new schools. It is more difficult to develop technology standards for modernization for the simple reason that there are already teachers in the classrooms, and they all do things a little bit differently than each other.

As an exercise, try to identify the front of each classroom in a school or building. For new classrooms this is simple; this is where the "teaching wall" is located. But for classrooms without a teaching wall, you can bet that the teachers have adjusted their classrooms for their own purposes. And there is no problem with them doing so—until you come back around and ask, "Where should we hang your new screen and projector?" If you ask each teacher, you will do each classroom differently. What if the teacher moves?—actually, we know the teacher will move, eventually. So the standard should state, "The screen and projector *shall* be installed at the front of the classroom"—and don't ask the teacher. You may still have a problem identifying the front of each classroom, but at least you will be free to make the decision to do it one way.

Site-Based Management and Educational Technology

This is a great management concept for school districts. Basically, principals get the final say. This is terrible for education technology. When extended to technology standards, this translates to "Each school is different." Which also translates to "There are no district-wide technology standards."

Technology standards should be district-wide. Only those initiatives that can be standardized district-wide should be called standards. Individual schools may have their own standards, and that is fine, but this will come back to haunt the IT and education technology departments forever.

Software Standards—If You Standardize It, You Own It

I've often met with school districts and asked, "What are your district software standards for curriculum?"

Most respond by listing the software being purchased at some of the sites. They give answers like "We use software X for math at these grade levels."

There is a difference between documenting current practice and developing a standard. Many schools approach this process backward—meaning they look at what the teachers are buying and using in the classroom, and then they say, "These are our standards." This process doesn't hold up, if we are to develop outcome-based curriculum objectives and then identify the applications that support curriculum objectives.

A technologist should be able to use the OSI model to develop a "top-down" approach. This would work except that, in education, there are at least two layers above the top layer. We have dubbed this the Extended Education OSI Model.

We might name these two layers, Curriculum Objectives (at the top) and Professional Development. If the education technology department can identify the top three layers (Curriculum Objectives, Professional

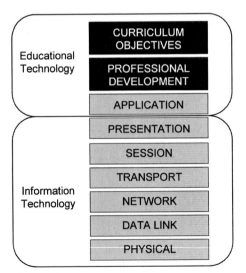

Figure 4.9.

Development, and Applications), then the IT department can assess the lower layers—all the way down to the physical layer (that is, how much more equipment, cabling, and infrastructure will be required to support the new curriculum focus).

The conversation then continues:

"Who paid for the software?"

"The site."

"Is the license up-to-date?"

"Yes, why, are you buying it for us now?"

Be careful of your step on this one. If you are developing a district standard for software, then licensing, maintenance, distribution, and training (professional development) are also your responsibility. You can bet that the site didn't license the software correctly, and certainly didn't get a site-license. But once your IT organization takes the lead on software, the licensing and updates are your headache now.

"Oh, maybe we don't need a standard for that."

Sustainable classroom technology standards are definitely one of the most important *Next* Practices.

ENTERPRISE MANAGEMENT AND SUSTAINABILITY

Sustainability—The ability to endure.

In IT, *sustainability* refers to any resource, process, or practice dedicated to supporting and maintaining systems and, ultimately, customer satisfaction. For a school district, there are two entities specifically tasked with technology sustainability: Education Technology and the IT department. These two entities should have the same goals and objectives but clearly delineated scope and scale of responsibility. There should also be a categorization of "Use" versus "Access" wherein "Use" refers to application of the features and functions of the software (education technology), and "Access" refers to the ability to run the software on the network, credentials, and so forth (IT).

The responsibility matrix in figure 4.10 will help identify and delineate scopes of responsibility.

Category	Description	Department
Instructional Software	Any and all software for desktops, labs, or classroom computers, including: - Math software - Science/Math tools - Reading tools	Educational Technology Curriculum Departments
Productivity	Productivity software : - Office - Publishing - Interactive Software - Collaboration Tools - Use	Educational Technology Curriculum Departments
	- Collaboration Tools – Access -	Information Technology Department
Student Information	SIS, Gradebook, Classroom Management - Use	Educational Technology
	SIS, Gradebook, Classroom Management – Access	Information Technology Department
Network Services	Electronic MailLibrary System	Information Technology Department
Network Equipment	Any software or applications tied to district/enterprise network: - Wired Connectivity - Wireless Connectivity - Internet Filter	Information Technology Department

Figure 4.10.

The IT Department

Your school district IT department should act like a corporate IT department (which is what it is). This sounds great, and important, but how does it apply to you?

Many small- to medium-size school districts are chronically under-staffed as compared to commercial organizations, especially if you take into account the number of computers, but that doesn't mean that they shouldn't operate like one. Large school districts typically have the opposite problem, but let's focus on the fundamentals.

The business of running a school district and fulfilling its information technology requirements is very similar to that of running a regionalized corporation with multiple remote sites, such as a regional bank with many small branches, or a hospital with many remote clinics. The district resembles a central office that has fewer overall users than the remote sites but houses centralized applications and has staff that supports operations in the remote sites.

This type of business requires industry-standard local area networks (LANs) at each site and a robust wide area network (WAN) with bandwidth requirements similar to that of other businesses of equal computer counts. A data center should house all mission-critical IT components and provide uninterruptible power and high-availability architectures to keep the enterprise running reliably through its business cycle (that is, all the time).

These days, WiFi should provide, at the very least, coverage, and at best, saturation, throughout each site.

Each site should also support secure guest/student WiFi as well. All district-wide applications should be collapsed back to the district data center and be protected by building environmental control (air conditioning and power), firewall, and security. Voice, paging, security and e-mail are all Internet-protocol (IP) based and centrally managed.

This description applies to the most progressive school IT environments. But the reality is that only within the last four to five years have all the technologies become available, at reasonable cost, to make this architecture achievable, especially for smaller districts.

So why wouldn't IT staffing and operations at school districts be modeled the same way as in a regional bank? Mostly it's because of the lack of formal IT strategic planning and enterprise management processes.

The problem becomes how to *document* that your department is understaffed—or more importantly, how to *determine* if your department is understaffed. This information is key to all IT organizations, in the public or private sector.

Right-sizing your IT department is a *Next* Practice.

In small districts, it is typical that the IT department is run by two to three people mastering all areas of IT, along with a smattering of techs supporting individual sites. Consultants and integrators are called in for escalation and projects.

The organization chart in figure 4.12 reflects most small- to medium-size school districts, up to about twenty schools.

The dotted-line relationship between principals and site techs tends to be traditional, while more progressive IT departments would have the techs centrally located and dispatched based on expertise to any remote site (of course, long distances may cause this model to vary).

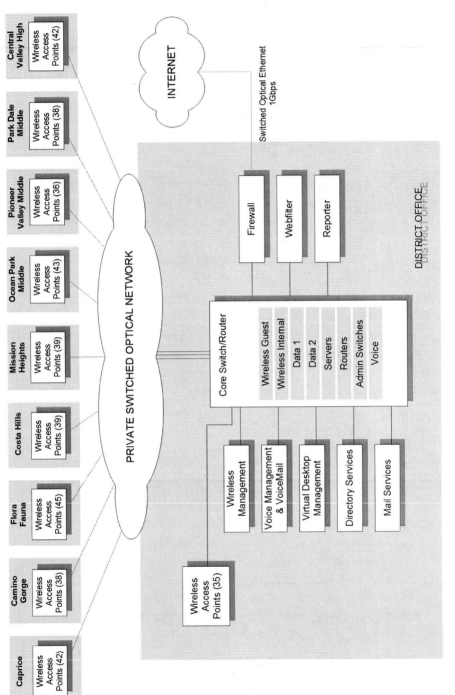

Figure 4.11.

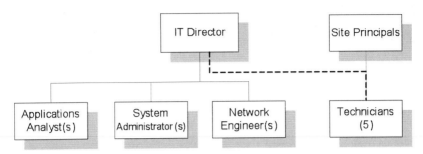

Figure 4.12.

However, this dotted line can pit site technicians against IT in some instances—that is, the needs of the individual site become more influential than centralized IT departmental processes and standards. How often has a site tech said, "I didn't ask her to create a ticket because I was standing right there."

But now the call-tracking system doesn't reflect the work done or the problem encountered. This information compiled and reported can become the key to trend analysis and future problem resolution, or even to problem mitigation. For instance, if the site tech always maps the network drive for each teacher, then the teachers will always be reliant on his availability. If they were all trained on drive mapping, this task would completely go away and the tech would be free to work on higher priority tasks. Of course, we know that some might see this as job security, while others would know this as a waste of time and resources.

The most important thing is for the district IT department to have the following roles and resources:

1. Information Technology Strategic Planning at or above the director level
2. IT Standard Organization Staffing Model
   a. Network/Security
   b. Systems/Services
   c. Applications
   d. Support/Maintenance
3. Help Desk/Call Tracking/Process Management
4. Enterprise Management Suite

Enterprise management and sustainability planning is a *Next* Practice.

TECHNOLOGY ROLES IN THE ORGANIZATION

Up to this point, we've discussed IT and education technology organizations within districts, as well as technical roles within each department. We've also touched briefly on the subject of strategy versus tactics.

To apply this principle to the organization, it is important to recognize the strategic or tactical scope of each role within the organization. What's curious is that these scopes are often flipped upside-down—meaning someone is making decisions outside their appropriate scope.

For example, the chief information officer (CIO) of a district asks a network engineer, "Okay, what do we need to add to next year's budget for IT?" Then the network engineer says, "We need 10 Gig and Enterprise VMware licenses." This stuff may be needed, but how does he know? What else might they need?

This process is absolutely backward. The CIO should be announcing to the department, "Okay, next year, we will need to support a minimum of ninety wireless devices in each classroom, and we'll need to move all our computer labs to virtual desktops. I need you to develop a budget estimate to do all the high schools in year 1, and the middle schools in year 2."

Here's another example of out-of-scope decision making. The CIO says, "We're going to install Apple TV in every classroom," when he should be asking his technical team, "What's the best way to stream broadcast television into each classroom?" See the difference?

We've introduced the Education Extended OSI Model for education technology. As noted, this model has two education-specific layers above the typical OSI model: curriculum objectives and professional development.

If we flip this model on its side, we are able to discuss the strategic versus tactical scopes of each of the departments.

Figures 4.13 and 4.14 show the scope of technology decision making within an organization. The two

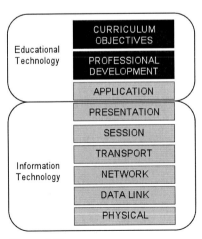

Figure 4.13.

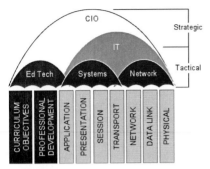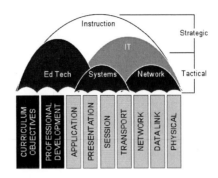

Figure 4.14

examples address an organization wherein the CIO is a cabinet-level entity, and one wherein the assistant superintendent of instruction represents both Education Technology and IT. You can see that the Education Technology role tends to take on a more strategic role when the superintendent of instruction represents both Education Technology and IT organizations.

Both of these models will work given departmental cooperation. The point is that strategic decisions need to be made at the cabinet level and that the departments develop the tactical implementation plans.

ENTERPRISE DESKTOP MANAGEMENT— ONE PLATFORM PLEASE

The ability to manage the enterprise is the biggest possible asset an IT department can have. Multiplatform installations require more than double the tech support.

This could be sticking my neck way out, and a lot of my friends at Apple will hate me, but the time has come to face the reality of Mac in the PC world. Mac enthusiasts have always been emotionally connected to their computing, while PC users tend to be more pragmatic and utilitarian.

These days, the devices are becoming even more innocuous and disparate. Any district looking toward a BYOD (bring your own device) model should really separate from dictating hardware standards for end-user devices—except for minimal compatibility, performance, and security standards.

Education, however, has long been the bastion of Macs, where they have been "accepted" as easier-to-use with better educational tools and, therefore, worth the cost differential. Steve Jobs made his mark with the Apples for Teachers program in the early 1980s.

Unfortunately, many IT trends have brought us to the point where we are today—the Mac can no longer fend-off the barbarians.

Here are some of the main factors.

Cost

More than ever, Netbooks and PC laptops are coming in at less than half the cost of an Apple MacBook. Schools cannot ignore the fact that twice as many student computing devices can be had for each Mac. As one-to-one initiatives and student laptops proliferate, this cost factor will become more and more obvious. Of course the iPad obscures this line of reasoning, but a whole new debate about tablets, smartphones, and other end-user devices really starts to complicate things. When you get right down to it, the IT department must focus on devices that it can manage at the enterprise level. Beyond this, a BYOD perspective will mitigate the need for an end-user device standard.

We recently purchased hundreds of laptops for one of my school districts. We outfitted two large high schools with Windows-based PC laptops, then spent an equal amount of money purchasing MacBooks for one middle school because they were "standardized on Macs"— paying more than double for the MacBooks than the student PC laptops. I even went to the effort of creating a report regarding standards, costs comparisons, and enterprise management systems. As much as I tried to make all aware of the gross imbalance of expenditure, the district went forward—that site-managed thing again.

Management

As hard as you try, it is still rare to find a school district that is able to manage all their Macs as well as their PCs in the active directory enterprise.

Sure, Apple says this can be done, and they'll send their pre-sales field engineers to tell you how, but the school districts that have done this successfully are few and far between. Do some Google searches, and you'll see some work-arounds, which is exactly what they are—enterprises don't manage well with "work-arounds."

Since there are no districts that have no PCs (at least I haven't encountered one), schools that purchase Macs are forced to support both platforms. Usually this means managing the PCs with group policy, and then adding third-party tools to attempt to do the same with the Macs. Oftentimes the Macs are not truly managed at all—or in the best cases, only at the site level. This is the biggest missed opportunity for an IT enterprise—the ability to truly manage all devices. Once again, however, the BYOD initiative will focus IT on devices they can control, then apply security and use standards that support everything else.

The soft dollars expended on multiplatform support can be mostly quantified by accumulating the payroll and materials cost of IT staffing and tools, but the soft-dollar cost of an inability to manage the whole enterprise is unquantifiable.

Enterprise network management is a key to sustainable IT operations and is a *Next* Practice.

THE CLOUD

"The Cloud" may be the most influential buzz-word for the 21st century in computing (so far). I won't define it for you because that's the whole point. It's there, but it isn't.

There's lots of talk about Cloud computing in school districts these days. But how does it affect yours?

Cloud computing is just another version of outsourced computing services. Only now, it's more scalable and easier to implement than ever.

I don't need to tell you to "Google it" if you want a complete explanation. Each provider has a different version of the same concept. One of the best packages available is from Amazon. Their Cloud computing services have everything, including virtual computing, networking, database, and e-commerce services. Yes, you could run all your K–12 and business applications on it.

But here's the salient business point: philosophically, Cloud computing is a "lease" in the old "lease-versus-buy" analysis. It's the question of capital equipment expenditure (and associated amortization/depreciation exercise) or operational expense.

Outsourcing of computing, networking, and database allows an organization to rely on very large companies to build disaster-proof data centers, highly available computing and storage models, and monitoring and management features that are based on service level agreements (SLAs). You've got to understand that Amazon can build it bigger, better, cheaper, and more powerful than your IT director and budget.

For small school districts, it's when the time comes to upgrade your servers, and develop a serious disaster recovery capability, that a cost analysis is called for. Then you will be hit with some real hard (and big) numbers. You'll then have a good incentive to do a lease-versus-buy analysis.

Now that we've established the fundamental benefit of the Cloud—the outsourcing of computing and capital equipment—we can note that the most unique benefit of the Cloud is elasticity.

In any IT architecture, a key objective is scalability—that is, the ability to grow, or scale-up, a platform without disrupting the core architecture. Elasticity becomes the ability to scale-up, or scale-down, computing capacity. Why? The most obvious example is seasonality, or business cycles.

For example, think about your SIS gradebook and reporting function come year-end. As the grading cycle gears up, computing resources need to scale up and expand to meet additional computing and storage requirements. But when summer comes, traditional IT architectures don't scale back down. School districts don't sell-off computing or storage capacity for the down-cycle. That capacity simply goes unused—which is another way of saying it is wasted. Organizations would love to be able to "sell" this capacity to others, but there is no marketplace for this capacity—except in the Cloud.

The Cloud can be elastic, allowing a school district to pay for compute "cycles" as requirements expand, and then, to pay less again during the down-cycle.

This totally unique computing phenomenon holds the secret to the Cloud's true power. And your first step, again, will be triggered by your next server upgrade.

There is one thing that you can be 100 percent sure of with Cloud computing—it costs money. It's never free, and it never will be free. Conversely, if you buy your own stuff, and keep it long enough, that equipment can be fully depreciated and in essence will have no recurring hard-dollar cost. But you also know—you will have to replace it by then anyway.

And therein lies the distinction between Cloud computing and traditional computing models: it is really an operational expense (OpEx) versus capital expense (CapEx) analysis.

Lease versus Buy

Remember the lease-versus-buy analysis you learned in Finance 101 (oh, you weren't a business major)? The one thing you learned for sure was that in real dollars, you pay a premium for financing. It isn't until you make the net present value (NPV) calculation that the analysis comes to equilibrium.

The analysis would be simple if you compared purchasing all the equipment yourself (including all the business continuity and disaster recovery components necessary to provide even mid-tier availability), against a Cloud-based services model. But the reality is that there is always a mixture, or hybrid solution presenting itself as another cost alternative. And soft-dollar costs become difficult to quantify unless you can account for dedicated staffing and resources.

The typical thought-process leading to Cloud-based solutions goes like this:

1. How much will it cost to buy the new servers, storage area network (SAN), and associated networking components for the new systems?
2. How much will it cost to add cabinets, power, and cooling to support this expansion in the data center? Wow, double?
3. What about if we just co-locate the equipment? That will give us unlimited expansion space, power, and cooling. The co-location will become a monthly operational cost, instead of a capital improvement cost.
4. But the equipment will no longer be on our premises. So?
5. Can we lease the equipment? Yes. Then we will still need to install, integrate, administer, and manage the equipment at the co-location facility.

6. Well, if we are leasing co-location facility space, and leasing hardware/software, and paying consulting fees for installation and integration, why don't we just pay for it monthly under these service-level agreements?
7. How much does that cost?

Operating Expense versus Capital Expense

The reality is, if you were to cost it all out for your own installation, the annualized operating expense (OpEx) is at a slight premium to your capital expense (CapEx) if you built it all yourself, support it with your own people, and depreciate the equipment over three to five years.

We did a recent cost analysis of our hosted solution. We own all our own servers, SANs, and network equipment, stored in a tier 4 co-location facility. The cost model for Cloud-based services is different for each vendor but roughly based on computing services and software services. If you thought about all the hardware and software licenses you'd need to purchase in the CapEx model, your OpEx model will have all the same components, scaled by the number of users/instances.

Service Levels

The service levels become key to your internal analysis. Compare your fully loaded staffing cost against an eight-hour-day, five-business-days-a-week (8-5) support level. If your current system goes down during the weekend, everyone pretty much waits until Monday to start working on the outage, except in larger districts. Add in overtime premiums and compare that differential to the 24-7 service level of a Cloud provider, and you won't even come close.

The Reality of Cost

However, you won't be able to build the same tier 4 facility as most Cloud providers. Nor will you be able to quantify the 24-7 management/administration service levels you have with your internal organization. Plus, you don't have to fire up a generator once a month, or fill it with diesel fuel (oh, you don't have a backup generator? That means a Cloud-based service level for 24-7 computing is offering you availability you cannot attain in-house).

The OpEx-versus-CapEx analysis will come down to district philosophy. What are the CBO and the board of education comfortable with in regard to traditional capital improvements, equipment depreciation, and asset value, versus leasing everything? Will the board allow the district an encumbrance longer than the superintendent's term?

An interesting final point: *Cloud computing* can be your Cloud, or someone else's Cloud, but it's still a *Next* Practice.

THE PHYSICAL LAYER—STANDARDIZE INFRASTRUCTURE

Classroom Drops

How many drops should we install in each classroom? This question is never easy to answer. First of all, it assumes some kind of major funding source, such as a technology bond, or new school construction.

In the past twenty years, I helped develop standards for classrooms with everything from 6 fibers and 12 copper drops in each classroom to, more commonly today, 5 drops in each classroom (2 in front, 2 in back, and 1 in the ceiling for wireless). However, even this efficient design runs into problems when implementing wireless saturation and video security.

The cost of over-cabling (installing more cabling than will ever be used) must be balanced against the cost of under-cabling (installing too few cables, requiring incremental cable installs after the fact).

For new building construction, it is always cheaper to have the builder include more drops before the walls are finished and painted than to go back and install incremental drops later. For modernization, each additional category 6 drop (dual) will likely cost an average of $750 to $1,000 per drop. New-construction drops will normally cost about $200 per drop. Take this into account as you develop your site-wide or district-wide cost estimates. Also, for wireless saturation, go ahead and put two drops in the ceiling for wireless; you're going to need it.

Backbone Fiber

In the 1990s, it was typical to install a certain number of multimode fiber and a certain number of single-mode fiber, the thought being that at a future date, the single-mode would be required to support higher bandwidths. Most of the single-mode installed for this reason has never been used.

Today, a new installation might only use single-mode fiber. The issue becomes convoluted in modernization. If the old standard was to install both, what should I do in new buildings connecting to the old backbone?

Single-mode fiber is incrementally more expensive than multimode, but what makes it more expensive to implement is the electronics. The multimode fiber interface uses LED (light emitting diode) technology while a single-mode fiber interface requires a laser. This is why single-mode has been typically utilized for long-haul applications.

For today's LAN standards, multimode fiber within two kilometers is still the most cost-effective. Keep in mind that disparate fibers cannot be connected to each other without active electronic equipment.

Video Security

When is it time to seriously look at video security for your school or district? Well, if you've been keeping your network up to snuff—meaning you've been implementing standards-based networking—then the time could be now. Every school district has multiple properties, labs full of equipment, and public safety as their responsibility.

Unfortunately, the most confusing time to implement video security is now because of the umpteen different technologies and providers. A simple call to ADT can have you set up in a day or two, but as with any other technology-based initiative, you have to take the time to plan—know your objectives, then plan accordingly. What is the point of setting up a video camera if there is no one to monitor it? Will you record and archive the video? How long will you keep it?

Let's look at objectives—two main reasons to implement video security are either (1) property protection, or (2) active monitoring. The former means that if someone comes on the property and does some damage or steals, you'll be able to go back into the video archive and see the perpetrator and possibly the crime. In this instance, the type and placement of cameras will become critical. The latter means that someone, or something, is monitoring the video and can activate alerts in the case of a security breach. You can see that unless your district is quite large and security is a big issue, like in a casino, you will probably not be doing active monitoring. Also, active monitoring is required to support any kind of people protection. Be careful not to connect one capability with the other. If your district assumes any type of personal protection with a video security system, your district's liability escalates.

Let's step back. Video security in today's IP-enabled world should be one part of a comprehensive security plan that includes access control, intrusion detection, and video surveillance.

A total system encompassing all three areas could conceivably aim cameras and trigger recording based on intrusion, and schedule door and perimeter access on preprogrammed schedules. Cameras could aim and monitor APs on this schedule and trigger alerts. Analytics could monitor images, record, trigger, light-up, and even call 911. But you can see how this comprehensive system could easily go cost-ballistic.

Next Complication—Technology

Although a completely IP-based system can be designed and implemented—and these systems can provide the best integration of capabilities—the cost of IP-based components is still higher than traditional CCTV-based systems. Plus, the need to upgrade structured cabling and networking components could drive the cost out the window.

Here's another one: How will all this streaming video affect your network utilization? This one could be crippling. Imagine twenty-five cameras streaming live, high-resolution video on your backbone network.

Many, many issues cloud this complex technology discipline. In fact, most video-security consultants have their roots and experience in one of these disciplines—security, CCTV, video, or now IT. But all these disciplines may be required in this comprehensive solution.

Finally, think of board policy. What is the district's responsibility and liability once the cameras are installed? What if a fight occurs in plain view of the cameras and the system is not working, or the camera resolution isn't high enough to identify perpetrators? Or what if the crime is recorded but no action is taken? There is also the issue of archival retention: how long shall archive data be kept? Does the state have minimum standards? Could those standards cause our minimal installation to go over budget? Let's relive the e-mail retention question times 100.

Networking

Just like the cabling balancing act, a similar exercise comes with the networking equipment. Shall you assume (and therefore purchase) enough network ports to activate every drop installed? In one installation, we installed twelve ports in every classroom and enough network switches to light up each port. However, bond funds could not be used for computers (in this instance), thus the school could only use existing computers during the first few years. Less than 8 percent of the copper and switch ports were utilized in this scenario.

Similarly, power-over-ethernet (POE) presents a similar dilemma. Voice over Internet protocol (VoIP) telephones and wireless access points require POE. Assumptions must be made to determine the number of POE ports required for each classroom/building.

Voice over Internet Protocol

Yes, VoIP is one of the hottest technology trends for school districts and businesses these days, but why? And is it right for your district?

First of all, VoIP is a protocol to support voice over a network. It really should be referred to as IP telephony. But more importantly, it provides the key to technology convergence—allowing the data network to become the central infrastructure for voice and data.

IP telephony uses a network server in place of a private branch exchange (PBX; a traditional phone system is a time-domain multiplexing private branch exchange, or TDM PBX). This new technology model eliminates the hardware limitations of TDM PBXs by supporting any number of IP telephone devices—limited only by software licenses. School districts with many remote sites no longer require a PBX at each remote location. One IP PBX can support the entire district via the wide-area network. This is the main capital cost advantage of IP telephony. Additionally, IP phones connect to the same network drops as the computers—no more separate networks for voice and data.

For some school districts, there is no real benefit derived from moving to IP telephony in the short-term. The phones cost more and require software licenses. If your district has fewer that fifty phones and telephone-based communication is not a big part of your operation, IP telephony may not be a good investment.

Districts with more than fifty phones are typically challenged to seek the benefits of IP telephony, a challenge usually triggered by the need to upgrade their current phone system. Most major phone-system manufacturers will sell their version of IP telephony. So you will be looking at IP telephony no matter what. This is the primary reason to look at IP telephony now—you will have to sooner or later, so better to do it on your schedule.

The main point to get from this is that unless your district is already dealing with this upgrade issue, your district is probably not going to benefit from IP telephony, in the near term. If this issue has already come up, then you will no longer be able to table this decision.

Once your current phone-system vendor tells you that their upgrade is VoIP, it will trigger a chain of questions such as Can I use my old phones? Can I use my current wiring? Is your system compatible with my network equipment? What about my fax machines?

Preparing for a new phone system can be a traumatic experience. Down-time, training, and compatibility are just a few of the issues to be dealt with.

There are, however, some litmus tests that can help you wade through some of the more difficult decisions.

First, is your current phone system at end-of-life, at end-of-support, or breaking down? If any of these descriptions hold, then your district needs to move to the next step.

Second, can your staff support a move to this new technology? Unfortunately, PBX support is much different from IP telephony support—the former is a wiring-and-PBX/voicemail technician, the latter, a network engineer with IP telephony training—big difference.

Next, can my organization support this change in the near term? If not, better submit a new organizational staffing request and plan to tackle this in the next fiscal year. Or possibly look to outsource implementation and support. Your current phone-support tech will give you the stink-eye unless he or she is also prepared for this shift—not likely. I've been called the "devil" because I was responsible for eliminating jobs by going to this new-fangled technology that does the same thing as the old phone system—nothing could be farther from the truth.

Finally, take all aspects into account. Sometimes your vendor will quote the upgrade with implementation, without telling you the cost of infrastructure upgrades (think structured cabling and network equip-ment) that will be required to support the new technology. What? I have to buy switches now, POE, UPSs?

Here's a basic checklist for IP telephony (VoIP) implementation:

- structured cabling
- routing/switching
- WAN connectivity between remote sites
- UPS systems in every closet (phones can't go down in a brown-out)
- PSTN requirements
- survivability
- auto-attendant
- voicemail
- dial-plan
- data center
- operations
- end-user training and support

If you don't know some of these terms and acronyms, more research on your part is due.

This is just the analysis; be prepared to perform a complete cost-benefit comparison as well.

It's not a simple exercise, but the benefits could easily outweigh the costs. Just do your homework.

Technology convergence is the last *Next* Practice.

Putting It All Together

You've been on quite a journey; we've covered a lot of material, some parts of it more technical than others, in a very short time. Now what do you do? Take a deep breath and let's review how *Next Practices* can guide you in making intelligent technology decisions. After all, the status quo is not what we are trying to achieve. *Best* practices are stagnating. That's where everyone else wants to go. You want to go beyond that and implement *next* practices in technology to support 21st-century learning. Here is a simple outline that will guide your way.

- Build a *Next* Practices Team
  The key role players who will help you successfully use technology in support of instruction are your superintendent, your assistant superintendent for curriculum and instruction, and your assistant superintendent of technology. Your school/district titles may be different, but the roles are the same. These key people, working together, and focusing on instruction and technologies to support instruction, will guide your school/district to successful implementations.
- Have a Plan
  Take the time and commit the resources to do strategic technology planning. Know and communicate the district priorities. Ensure that your key staff are all on the same page and are focused on those priorities. This may best be done by asking someone outside your organization to guide you through this strategic process. Make sure that your technology department is strategic to the

organization and not just a maintenance organization. Ensure that this department sits at the cabinet level of your school district.

- Have a Laser-Focused Curriculum
  Everyone in your organization should know what the curriculum focus is in your district. Everything about successful technology integration depends on this *Next* Practice. If you're not there yet, stop and get there before taking on any technology integration efforts.
- Be Smart about Curriculum Initiatives
  Next Practices centers on curriculum and the technology that supports your curriculum focus. One-to-one technology initiatives almost always miss the mark. They tend to be technology for technology's sake, and solutions looking for problems. If you do this right, your initiative will not be about technology, it will be about creating a one-teacher-to-one student model.
- Be Smart about Technology Purchases
  Next Practices doesn't mean the latest whiz-bang gadget. *Next* Practices focuses on what works to support curriculum—technologies that have proven themselves to support your curriculum efforts through the pilot and standardization process.

  Calculate the total cost of ownership (TCO) for any new technology.

  - Operationalize your technology budget. Lease where it makes sense. Technology should be a line item in your budget. Stop the yo-yo spending.
  - Ensure that there is executive sponsorship of technology and applications that support your focused curriculum.

- Build an Infrastructure to Support Technology
  Next Practices is about understanding what the curriculum efforts of the district are and ensuring that an infrastructure is in place to support those efforts. You don't want to have a failure to launch because you neglected to take care of your infrastructure needs. If you're not sure how to do this, it is money well spent to have someone help your organization with this critical task.

- Design Sustainability into Your Support Organizations
  The education technology department and the information technology department must work hand in hand to support the overall organization within their designated scopes and be able to escalate, hand off, and manage problems through resolution as a single entity with a single customer base. *Next* Practices is about providing technology leadership to manage the enterprise for the long-term achievement of district objectives.
- Measure What You Do
  Next Practices are constantly evolving. Unless you are evaluating, measuring, and tuning your practices, you may miss the *next* evolution.

About the Authors

Darryl Vidal has been consulting for schools implementing technology for over twenty years and has a bachelor's degree in information management. He started his technical career installing ethernet networks at Hughes Aircraft and other aerospace firms in the early 1980s. After working at Apple Computer with education accounts in the late '80s, he began technical consulting for school districts. His projects have included district-wide implementations of VoIP, wireless, desktop and data center virtualization, and video security. His primary instructional focus for over fifteen years has been the ever-evolving technology classroom. Mr. Vidal has developed the formal strategic planning and project management methodology known as MAPit. He is currently vice president and principal education technology consultant for Southern California–based consultancy Networld Solutions.

Michael Casey has over thirty years of experience in education as a classroom teacher, educational technology resource teacher, program manager for educational technology, and executive director for information technology at San Diego Unified School District. Mr. Casey has taught chemistry, physics, mathematics, and computer science at the secondary levels. He also taught at the university level at San Diego State University and the University of California, San Diego Extension College. His accomplishments include enterprise implementations of enterprise resource planning (ERP) solutions in human resources; finance; supply chains; student information systems; data warehousing; Microsoft Collaboration Tools; video conferencing; and enterprise wireless and special-education solutions. He is nationally recognized for successful ERP implementations and has reviewed numerous implementations for the Council of the Great City Schools. He is currently the director of technology for Del Mar Union Schools and the president and CEO of Eire Group, a technology-consulting solutions group.